THE DRUKNEN COOBOOK

Milton Crawford

Clarkson Potter/Publishers
New York

Copyright © 2013 by Milton Crawford
Figure illustration copyright © 2013 by Max Baxter
Food illustration copyright © 2013 by Katie Morgan

Published in the United States by Clarkson Potter/Publishers, an imprint
of the Crown Publishing Group, a division of Random House LLC,
a Penguin Random House Company, New York.
www.crownpublishing.com
www.clarksonpotter.com

CLARKSON POTTER is a trademark and POTTER with colophon is a
registered trademark of Random House LLC.

Originally published in Great Britain by Square Peg, an imprint of
The Random House Group Limited, London, in 2013.

Library of Congress Cataloging-in-Publication Data
Crawford, Milton.
  The drunken cookbook / Milton Crawford.
     pages cm
  1. Cooking (Liquors) 2. Quick and easy cooking. 3. Food and wine pairing.
4. Drinking of alcoholic beverages—Humor. I. Title.
  TX726.C73 2014
  641.6'2—dc23
                              2013050371

ISBN 978-0-8041-8517-2
eBook ISBN 978-0-8041-8518-9

Printed in China

Cover design by Jim Massey
Design by Make Ready Studio & Matt Baxter

10 9 8 7 6 5 4 3 2

First American Edition

If you're struggling to read this, then you probably shouldn't be trying to cook.

Alcohol diminishes our inhibitions. It makes us more likely to be adventurous; to speak to someone we wouldn't normally speak to, do something we normally wouldn't do, go somewhere we normally wouldn't go. It tempts us to redefine the limits we unconsciously ring-fence our lives with: to abandon caution, to speak honestly rather than gloss over the truth, to extend metaphors beyond the pale. In other words, alcohol offers, however dishonestly, a taste of freedom, which is one of the reasons it can be so dangerously addictive. It also offers the opportunity for other forms of experimentation and adventure in different areas of our lives—and, for the purposes of this book, I'll mainly be talking about the kitchen.

Whether it be on returning home from the pub after a quick drink with colleagues on a weekday, or having invited friends 'round at 3 a.m. after a hard night on the tiles, the tipsy gastronome has the opportunity to explore tastes and flavors that he might previously have dismissed, but that now suddenly make more sense.

Intensity is important—the dipsomaniacal gourmet embraces strong, bold flavors: salty, smoky, spicy, unctuous, and garlicky. We are interested in umami and pickles, the sharp slice of raw onion cutting through cheese, the powerful punch of chili spiking pork fat. It may be a little crude, but then the inspiration for these recipes comes from bar snacks, street food, and takeaways rather than Michelin-starred restaurants—food that is prepared quickly to deliver a big and satisfying hit.

Practicality also has to play a role: the recipes contained within this book are designed to be simple enough for a person who is moderately incapacitated, and quick enough to prepare before the eyes glaze over. Safety is also a consideration—deep-fried food has not been included, for example.

But this is not just a cookbook for complete inebriates, whose compass is not aligned with their mentis (whatever the hell that is). They are already well catered for by kebab shops, curry houses, and chip shops. This is more a playful tome for all kinds of gastronomic adventure; alcohol is the schooner for our voyage on the seas of culinary creativity, booze is our boat across oceans of bacchanalian kitchen-craft . . .

Now, what was I saying about extending metaphors . . . ?

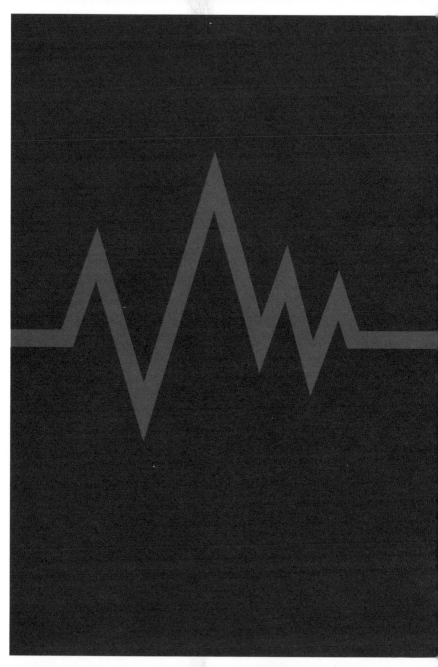

WHAT'S THE DRUNKEN DIAGNOSIS?

—

Are you three
sheets to the
wind, or have
the sheets blown
away entirely?

Hint: if you've no idea what I'm talking about,
drop the book right now and walk away.

Use this handy diagnostic section to work out if you're a bubble or a newt, a puppy or a penguin. This will help you determine which recipes you may be able to tackle. It will be easier and more accurate (and more fun) if a companion is on hand to adjudicate, as your own judgment may be less than objective. The tests all assume that some level of drinking has taken place. Complete sobriety does not register on the scale, so teetotalers, please close the book and consider instead giving it to that uncle who always seems rather too eager to pour a G&T at four in the afternoon.

THE ONE-LEGGED STANDING TEST

—

Instead of simply administering a breath test, some sadistic American cops like to humiliate potential drunk-drivers by making them do all kinds of ridiculous gymnastics at the side of the road while other drivers cruise by, laughing at the circus unfolding on the sidewalk. You may choose your own audience while you do this test. Regardless of the results, please do not consider driving afterwards.

Stand with your hands by your sides and raise one foot (either will do) approximately 6 inches above the ground in front of you. While holding this position, look at the ceiling and count to 30.

How long did you last?

(a) the full distance
(b) the mid-twenties
(c) how long would you like me to last?
    Okay, yes, I admit, the mid-teens
(d) under 10
(e) how did you balance? Wobble, wobble
(f) aahhhh! Thud

THE REFLEX RULER TEST

—

As you get more and more drunk, your reflexes get poorer and poorer. Even with relatively low blood-alcohol levels from just a couple of drinks, your reflexes are half as good as they were when you were sober. There is an easy way to check the quality of your reflexes that you may remember from school: the reflex ruler test. You will need a standard 12-inch ruler and someone to administer this test.

Your partner will need to hold the ruler vertically at approximately shoulder height. Hold out your hand approximately 4 inches below the bottom of the ruler. (Depending on the punctiliousness of your partner, he or she may decide to measure this precisely.) Position your finger and thumb so that you are ready to grasp the ruler should it fall (it will, shortly).

Your partner should ask: "Are you ready?"

Once you have replied in the affirmative, he or she may drop the ruler. Your task is to catch it as quickly as possible between your finger and thumb. Technically you should do this a few times to rule out freak results and take the average.

How many inches did the ruler drop before you caught it?

(a) fewer than 4 inches
(b) 4–6 inches
(c) as Einstein said: "Not everything that counts can be counted, and not everything that can be counted counts." If I have to put a figure on it: 6–8 inches?
(d) 8–12 inches
(e) I used that ruler to measure the distance between my eyes
(f) what ruler?

3

THE
MEMORY
TEST

—

Neural function declines in all kinds of ways due to the presence of alcohol in the bloodstream. One obvious symptom is memory recall. What was the name of that film? Who was that person you both knew at school? Who passed out on the pavement after that party?

Test how much your memory has deteriorated by playing a game of Granny Goes to Market. You'll need someone to play it with. You know this game? All you have to do is to say "Granny goes to market and she bought. . . ." Then you begin listing the items that Granny picked up, taking turns with your companion(s), one at a time. It could be anything, so it might go: an apple, a ball of wool, a clamshell, a dog, an Ecstasy pill, a fennel bulb, a gigolo, a hammer, an iguana. . . . The items do not have to be in alphabetical order. I just did that because I thought it was funny (as I write this I've drunk three pints of Guinness and an espresso martini). The person who can remember the most items wins.

How many items could you remember?

(a) 10–15
(b) 8–10
(c) as Mark Twain said: "If you tell the truth, you don't have to remember anything." Okay, somewhere between 5 and 8
(d) fewer than 5, I think
(e) who the hell is Granny?
(f) bleurrgh

THE
MOOD
TEST

—

One symptom of drunkenness is what is called the "labile mood," sometimes called "emotional dysregulation," or, to you and me, mood swings. You might recognize this from that person who is perfectly nice when he's sober, but can suddenly become a monster when he's drunk.

This primitive little test attempts to assess how balanced (or unbalanced) your mood is right now. Someone insults you. It's not a terrible insult. It's along the lines of: "You bloody idiot." Or: "You know what, you really are a bit of a loser." Or: "I'm really not sure about that cardigan." Something like that.

What's your reaction?

(a) come on, life's too short to be nasty to one another
(b) I love being me; if you got to know me, I'm sure you'd love me too
(c) Sir (or Madam), may I say: you seem to be speaking an infinite amount of nothing
(d) forget about it: give us a hug and let's party!
(e) get me another drink!
(f) come here: I'm going to f___ you up.

THE RESULTS

—

If you've
made it this
far, then
well done …

. . . it already suggests that you're not too horrendously smashed to manage basic tasks in the kitchen. But read on to find out the official diagnosis and how capable I feel you may be of tackling some proper cooking. When sharp knives and hot water are involved, it's probably best not to overextend yourself, so please err on the side of caution, rather than adventure.

The
Bubble

If you answered mainly (a) then you are probably experiencing "The Bubble."

You have barely moved beyond sobriety but have imbibed just enough to have all the lightness and fizz of a bubble rising inexorably upwards in a flute of champagne. You are tinged with rose-tinted euphoria, warmed by the joy of humanity, buoyed by the oxygen of life. The glass is half full.

Depending on your sober abilities, you should be capable of making most recipes.

The
Puppy

If you answered mainly (b) then it's quite likely that right now you're "The Puppy."

Puppies are generally so full of confidence that everyone they meet instantly falls in love with them. You are in this puppy-like state at the moment, thinking that you are irresistibly charismatic/charming/beautiful/handsome (choose any or all of the above). In fact, your coordination and reflexes are already suffering, even though your senses feel extraordinarily heightened.

You should be able to make most recipes and, indeed, may feel as though it's all a bit too easy. But watch out—overconfidence can also be a significant handicap to success.

The
Oscar

If you answered mainly (c) then you're quite clearly in a state I describe as "The Oscar."

"Champagne for my real friends, real pain for my sham friends." Oscar Wilde was full of such witty asides, and by now you feel as though Wilde would struggle to keep up with your own brand of sparkling conversation. You're so sharp right now that people might cut themselves on you. Or, at least, that's what you think, as you are also beginning to slur a little and not everyone might be as impressed with your wit as you so evidently are.

If you are ready to take time out from talking, then you could attempt some of the easy to medium-difficulty recipes—but you may have a problem concentrating on some of the more difficult ones.

The
Duracell

If you answered mainly (d) then the evidence suggests you're "The Duracell."

A primal energy has been unleashed within you and now you are an unstoppable force of nature that is prepared to party for as long as it takes to . . . well, who knows what—there is neither rhyme nor reason to your incorrigibility. The difficulty is that this energy lacks coordination and sudden enthusiasms are forgotten as quickly as they came to you in the first place. Hang on, come back! This is for you. Right, now don't start making something to eat then give up halfway through.

Stick to the easiest of the recipes. and think about getting someone to help you.

BLAH BLAH BLAH BLAH BLAH BLAH

The
Penguin

If you answered mainly (e) then it seems that you may be "The Penguin."

As you become afflicted with a bunch of terms that can be found near the beginning of any reputable medical dictionary (agraphia, apraxia, ataxia), you may acquire that same kind of unsteadiness witnessed in the flightless birds of the southern hemisphere as they waddle through snowdrifts and ice, occasionally falling flat on their sleek bellies. Whereas real penguins are able to slide effortlessly along on their tummies, though, you will most likely find yourself stranded, and, quite probably, in some pain.

It may be that toast is the best thing you can turn your hand to right now. Any more than that and toast may be what you'll become.

The
Newt

If you answered mainly (f) then I reckon you're "The Newt."

Detailed investigation usually reveals compelling reasons for the origins of seemingly obscure phrases, but "pissed as a newt" remains somewhat enigmatic. Something is clear: the newt means you have plumbed the depths. You will not be able to read these sentences. They are lost on you. I have literally wasted minutes writing words that will be incomprehensible to my readers. Now I know how Will Self and Salman Rushdie must feel.

The
Tipsy Store
Pantry

It's good to have a range of "super-ingredients" on hand so that you can quickly inject serious flavor into your food when you most need it.

Here are suggestions for some store-cupboard staples:

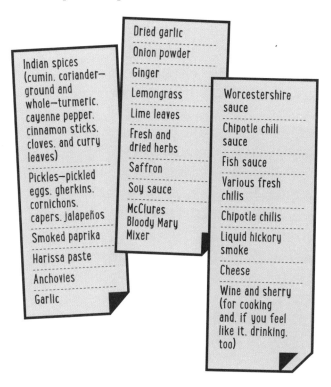

Indian spices (cumin. coriander—ground and whole—turmeric. cayenne pepper. cinnamon sticks. cloves. and curry leaves)

Pickles—pickled eggs. gherkins. cornichons. capers. jalapeños

Smoked paprika

Harissa paste

Anchovies

Garlic

Dried garlic

Onion powder

Ginger

Lemongrass

Lime leaves

Fresh and dried herbs

Saffron

Soy sauce

McClures Bloody Mary Mixer

Worcestershire sauce

Chipotle chili sauce

Fish sauce

Various fresh chilis

Chipotle chilis

Liquid hickory smoke

Cheese

Wine and sherry (for cooking and. if you feel like it. drinking. too)

The Recipes

THE DRUNKEN CARNIVORE
—

STEAMING HOT
—

WELL-OILED
—

SLOSHED STARCH
—

PLASTERED
PARTY FOOD
—

Bacon and chive
mini-röstis 100

Baked Camembert with
rosemary, thyme, and
soldiers 102

Bruschetta with olives
and anchovies 104

Crostini with tuna and
caper berries 106

English cheese fondue
with perry 108

Steak haché sliders on
toasted brioche 110

VITTLES
AND VINE
—

A simplified Arnold Bennett
omelette with white
Burgundy 130

Curried monkfish and mussels
with Gewürztraminer 132

Salt cod croquettes with
manzanilla 134

Seared scallops, smoked
lardons, and blood sausage
with porter 136

Stuffed grilled mussels with Innis
and Gunn Blonde 138

Venison sausages with cider
sauce and scrumpy 140

BOOZY
DESSERTS
—

Crêpes Tom Foster 116

Caramelized rum mango with
vodka lime Jell-O and
gingersnap crumble 118

Milton's tipsy trifle 120

Panettone with Pedro Ximénez,
raisins, almonds, and ice cream 121

Sherry and ginger log with
pistachio and chocolate 122

The Big Lebowski sundae 124

All recipes are for two people,
unless otherwise stated. All
recipes call for sea salt and freshly
ground black pepper, unless
otherwise stated.

Kitchens can be dangerous places
(please see the disclaimer absolving the author
of any responsibility for injury or health
problems that may arise from your efforts).
So these helpful icons indicate some of
the potential risks of injury you may face.

Boiling   Grater   Hot   Hot pan   Sharp
water   oven / grill   knives

In order to try and ensure that you don't
bite off more than you can chew, I have rated each
recipe in terms of the difficulty and/or effort involved
in making it. A recipe may be rated "difficult" not
because of any particular technical skill that is
required, but simply because there are quite a number
of different processes involved. These ratings make
the assumption that you might be somewhat
impaired in your capacity, but nonetheless you
should be realistic about what you attempt.

(cinch)   (fussy)   (toil)
[easy]   [moderate]   [difficult]

THE DRUNKEN CARNIVORE

If alcohol has the capacit
of our most primal lusts
why char-grilled meat—a
cavemen—is so prominen
barbecue to a man who
will show you his shiniest
the barbecued steak, anc
natural partners for a dri
one, and, of course, they
machismo of drinking. H
this kind of über-mascul
more metrosexual kind of
bi, and transgender ca
around the fire with th
shoulders and legs of m
grubby hands: cavepeo

o awaken within us some
nen perhaps this explains
d favored by all reputable
n drunken menus. Show a
s had a few beers and he
ile. The ubiquitous kebab,
rilled chicken seem to be
ng session, or the end of
re part and parcel of the
ever, I personally eschew
ty. This is an altogether
okbook: cavewomen, gay,
people should all gather
steaks and chops and
t grasped firmly in their
of the world, unite!

CHAR-GRILLED SMOKY HARISSA CHICKEN

WITH FRIED COUSCOUS
AND HERBS

———

     (fussy)

FOR THE CHICKEN: *4 boneless skinless chicken thighs ~ 1 tbsp lemon juice ~ 1 tsp salt ~ 1 tbsp harissa paste ~ 2 tbsp thick Greek yogurt ~ 1 tsp liquid hickory smoke ~ 1 tbsp olive oil ~ handful of finely chopped fresh mint leaves*
FOR THE COUSCOUS: *1 cup couscous ~ 1 tbsp olive oil ~ 2 onions, halved and thinly sliced ~ 1 tsp cumin ~ good handful of mint, finely chopped ~ good handful of parsley, finely chopped ~ handful of chives, finely chopped ~ few sprigs of oregano, roughly chopped ~ 2 tbsp lemon juice ~ salt, to taste*
TO SERVE: *lemon wedges ~ handful of mint leaves, finely chopped*

Harissa is one of my favorite ingredients: unlike many other chili products, it has a delicious deep, unctuous sweetness to it, as well as heat, that immediately conjures, to my mind at least, the southern (i.e., North African) side of the Mediterranean. The couscous, filled with fresh herbs, is a perfect accompaniment.

Milton's Method ☞ Place the chicken thighs between 2 pieces of plastic wrap and flatten out a little with a rolling pin to about ¼ inch thick.

Prick the chicken thighs with a knife. Place them in a bowl and sprinkle with the lemon juice and salt.

In a separate bowl, combine the harissa, yogurt, liquid hickory smoke, olive oil, and mint. Mix well and pour over the chicken.

Place the couscous in a saucepan and pour just enough boiling water over the couscous to cover it. Cover and leave for 10 minutes until the couscous has absorbed all the water.

Heat a frying pan over medium-high heat and add the olive oil. Cook the onions, stirring regularly, for 8–12 minutes until golden. Add the cumin, stir, then add the couscous. Keep stirring for 3–4 minutes until the couscous has absorbed most of the oil and started to turn golden. Lower the heat, add the herbs, lemon juice, and salt, stir again, and remove from the heat.

Heat the broiler and place the chicken on a wire rack above a rimmed baking sheet, a few inches below the broiler. Broil until the chicken is golden brown. Turn and broil the other side until it is cooked through, about 10 minutes in total.

Serve with wedges of lemon and a scattering of finely chopped mint leaves.

CHEAT'S CASSOULET

———

     (toil)

1 tbsp olive oil ~ 1½ tbsp butter ~ 4 boneless chicken thighs ~ 4 sausages, chopped into 1-inch pieces ~ 4 oz diced bacon/lardons ~ 1 onion, finely chopped ~ 3 cloves garlic, finely chopped ~ ⅓ cup red wine ~ 6 large tomatoes, diced ~ 1 15-oz can cannellini beans, drained and rinsed ~ 1 tsp finely chopped thyme ~ couple of sprigs of rosemary ~ 1 cup chicken stock ~ salt and pepper, to taste ~ 2 tsp cornstarch ~ 1 cup very coarse white bread crumbs **TO SERVE:** *frisée lettuce salad*

I remember camping on a small island off the coast of Brittany with a female friend of mine a few years ago and pretty much the only thing on this island was a boulangerie and just about all we had with us was some tins of cassoulet and a little camping stove. We lived off tinned cassoulet and baguettes (and copious amounts of red wine, of course) for about five days, swimming on deserted beaches and circumnavigating our newfound kingdom. It was paradise.

The traditional cassoulet takes a long time to cook, especially with confit duck legs, so I have tried to simplify it somewhat—it is, after all, an uncomplicated, rustic dish that's basically meat with baked beans. This is one-pot cooking at its best.

Milton's Method ☞ Heat the oven to 350°F. Heat the olive oil and butter in a large, heavy Dutch oven over medium-high heat and brown the chicken thighs all over. Take them out and set aside. Add the sausage and bacon to the Dutch oven and cook until golden. Add the onion, cooking and stirring until it becomes translucent, then add the garlic. Add the red wine, let the alcohol evaporate and the liquid reduce, then add the tomatoes, beans, thyme, and rosemary.

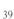

Stir and mash the tomatoes with the back of your spoon until they soften and start to create a thick sauce. Add the stock, season, and bring to boil. In a separate bowl, mix the cornstarch with a little water and add it to the pot. Stir, turn down the heat, and leave to simmer for 15 minutes with the lid off, stirring occasionally. The liquid should reduce and thicken further. Check the seasoning and return the chicken thighs to the Dutch oven, sprinkle the bread crumbs over the top, and place in the oven.

Leave it to cook for 1½ hours, or until the bread crumbs are golden and form a nice crust. Serve with a frisée lettuce salad.

CHICKEN LIVERS, BACON, AND MUSHROOMS ON TOAST

WITH CREAMY MUSTARD
AND MADEIRA SAUCE

—

1½ tbsp butter ~ 1 tbsp olive oil ~ 4 oz smoked lardons or diced bacon ~ 2 tbsp very finely chopped shallots ~ ½ lb baby portobello mushrooms, cleaned and sliced ~ 1 lb chicken livers ~ ¼ cup Madeira wine or medium sherry ~ 1 tbsp whole-grain mustard ~ handful of parsley, finely chopped ~ ½ cup heavy cream ~ salt and pepper, to taste ~ 4 slices ciabatta, toasted

Chicken livers and mushrooms, with their complementary but entirely different rich, earthy flavors, are two ingredients that seem to go naturally together. I became rather obsessed with mushrooms after I took a house in the New Forest for a while and fell in love with some varieties of fungi that I had never tried before, such as parasols and blewits. For this recipe, though, I am sticking with the regular baby portobello mushrooms that can be bought from any supermarket or greengrocer. Call me a philistine, but I prefer my chicken livers just cooked through rather than pink. If you prefer them pink then reduce the cooking time slightly.

Milton's Method ☞ Heat the butter and olive oil in a nonstick frying pan over medium-high heat. When the fat is warm, add the bacon and cook until it has begun to crisp up a little. Add the shallots and sauté for a couple of minutes until they have taken on a little color. Add the mushrooms and cook for 5 minutes or so, stirring regularly, until they have also taken on some color and released some of their moisture. Add the livers and cook for a further couple of minutes, then add the Madeira. Allow the alcohol to evaporate and the liquid to reduce for a couple of minutes, then stir in the mustard and half the parsley. Slowly add the cream, and season to taste.

Reduce the heat to medium-low and leave to simmer for 3–4 minutes, stirring occasionally, until the sauce has thickened. Taste for seasoning and adjust as required.

Serve on the toasted ciabatta slices with the remaining parsley sprinkled on top, and eat immediately.

THE PHILLY CHEESESTEAK SANDWICH

—

2 cloves garlic, crushed or finely chopped ~ 2 tbsp mayonnaise ~ 2 large, soft "sub" rolls or 1 French baguette ~ 2 tbsp olive oil ~ 1 large onion, halved and thinly sliced ~ 1 green bell pepper, deseeded and thinly sliced ~ ½ lb wafer-thin slices of steak ~ salt and pepper, to taste ~ ½ lb provolone, Gouda, or Monterey Jack cheese, thinly sliced

This is an all-American, thinly shaved fried steak served in a soft roll with cheese, peppers, and onion. Yes, a kebab with cheese. It'll feel like you've died and gone to heaven. Some people suggest freezing the steak before you slice it so that you can cut the slices especially thin. I don't consider this necessary.

Milton's Method ☞ Combine the garlic and the mayo in a small bowl. Split open your rolls or baguette and spread the garlic mayo inside.

Heat a nonstick frying pan over moderate heat and add half the olive oil. Add the onion and bell pepper and sauté for 5–6 minutes until the pepper has softened and the onion has taken on a little color.

Put the vegetables in a bowl, turn up the heat, add the remaining olive oil to the same pan and then the steak. Season the steak generously with salt and pepper, then stir it with a wooden spatula, pressing down as you go to break down the pieces of beef into smaller bits. Cook until the meat has browned, just a couple of minutes.

Take the pan off the heat and stir in the onion and bell pepper. Divide the mixture between your rolls and add the sliced cheese on top. For extra meltedness, pop into a warm oven for a couple of minutes then serve straightaway.

SEARED RARE
BEEF TENDERLOIN

WITH PARMESAN, ARUGULA,
AND AGED BALSAMIC VINEGAR

—

2 tbsp olive oil ~ 2 tbsp aged balsamic vinegar ~ salt and pepper, to taste~
1 lb beef tenderloin (thick end) ~ 2 cups arugula ~ 5 oz Parmesan or pecorino ~
⅓ cup green olives, pitted and thinly sliced

The most important part of this dish is searing the beef properly—
this is what will create the delicious, caramelized meat flavor.
In order to achieve it, you'll ideally want to have a cast-iron ridged
griddle pan that will need about as much heat as you can give it.
This level of heat creates its own risks—make sure that only the
beef is in contact with the pan and not any part of your own anatomy.
This is one for sharing—you'll need a fillet of about a pound, which
should make enough for 4 people. Try to get a fillet that has some fat
marbling in it.

Also, don't stint on the balsamic—cheap, thin vinegar will not
help. You will need to splash out a little on this.

Milton's Method ☞ Preheat the oven to 425°F and get your ridged
griddle pan onto the stove over high heat.

While the griddle pan is heating up, make a dressing from the
olive oil and 1 tablespoon of the balsamic and rub this into the fillet.
Season with salt and a little pepper and make sure this is massaged
into the meat evenly.

Once the griddle pan is very hot, start searing the beef so that it gets nice dark brown char marks all over. This should take 2–3 minutes.

Once the meat has been charred all over, place the fillet in a roasting pan and pop it into the oven—10 minutes will keep it rare, 12 minutes should be medium-rare, and after 14 minutes it will be increasingly well done. Remove from the oven and leave in the pan to rest for 5 minutes.

Place the arugula on a plate, slice the beef (into roughly ½-inch-thick slices), then shave the Parmesan on top, drizzle with the remaining balsamic vinegar, and garnish with the thinly sliced olives.

SPICY THAI-STYLE PORK BURGERS

WITH A CUCUMBER
AND PEANUT SALAD

———

FOR THE BURGERS: *1 or 2 hot Thai red chilis with seeds, thinly sliced ~ 2 cloves garlic, thinly sliced ~ 1 stick of fresh lemongrass, very thinly sliced ~ handful of cilantro (stalks and leaves), roughly chopped ~ 4 lime leaves, thinly sliced ~ ½-inch chunk of ginger, finely grated ~ 2 scallions, thinly chopped ~ ¾ lb bulk sausage ~ 2 oz bacon, cut into small pieces ~ 1 tbsp soy sauce ~ peanut or vegetable oil, for frying* **FOR THE CUCUMBER SALAD:** *1 cucumber ~ ½ red onion, very thinly sliced ~ 2 scallions, thinly sliced ~ 1 red chili, deseeded and thinly sliced ~ small handful of mint leaves, finely chopped ~ 3 tbsp peanuts, dry-roasted and lightly crushed* **FOR THE SALAD DRESSING:** *½ tsp shrimp paste ~ juice of ½ lime ~ 1 tbsp fish sauce ~ 1 tsp sugar ~ 1 tbsp soy sauce ~ 1 clove garlic, crushed* **TO SERVE:** *hamburger buns ~ Thai sweet chili sauce*

This is a great mix of sticky, fatty pork burgers brought to life with chili, lime leaves, lemongrass, and garlic, along with a zingy, refreshing cucumber salad. It's perfect on a hot day with a cold beer when you could put the burgers straight on to the grill and serve in a hamburger bun with Thai sweet chili sauce and the salad as a side. The other way of serving these burgers is by mixing some cooled rice noodles with the cucumber salad and popping the burgers on top.

This is at the simple end of the burger scale—because of the amount of pork fat binding everything together, there's very little chance that your burger will fall apart so there's no need to use a binder like eggs. Beware of getting chili in your eyes.

Milton's Method ☞ Whizz the chilis, garlic, lemongrass, cilantro, lime leaves, ginger, and scallions together in a food processor until the mixture is very fine and well combined. It should smell fantastic. In a large bowl, combine this mixture with the sausage meat and the bacon. Add the soy sauce and mix everything together very thoroughly. This is best done with your hands. Put the mixture in the fridge so that the pork meat can take on some of the flavor of the aromatic ingredients.

To prepare the salad, first halve the cucumber lengthwise, then cut each half lengthwise again a few more times, so you have about 6 long strips, then cut these in half lengthwise. Combine the cucumber and all the other salad ingredients, except the peanuts, in a large bowl.

Make the dressing by first putting the shrimp paste in a bowl and adding the lime juice. Stir this until it is blended together in a more liquid paste, then add the other ingredients. It will taste rather intense, but don't worry; the water in the cucumber will dilute the dressing somewhat. Adjust the amount of lime juice/sugar to taste. Gently toast the peanuts to release their flavor by dry-frying them for a couple of minutes over medium heat.

Wet your hands to shape the burgers—there should be enough for 4 good-sized burgers. Heat a splash of peanut or vegetable oil in a heavy frying pan over medium-high heat and add the patties once the oil is hot. Cook for about 5 minutes on each side, until the burgers are sticky and golden brown on the outside and cooked through. Add the peanuts and the dressing to the salad and toss well.

Serve immediately in hamburger buns with the crunchy cucumber salad and Thai sweet chili sauce on the side.

STEAMING
HOT

—

Curry is a common c
on the claret. Spic
the befuddled palat
tongues. Sensory ov
effect that we're after
do we go and sit quie
on life? No: that's wh
for. After a drink c
lights and loud co
dancing and fumblin
kisses. Spicy food
valent: bright, bras

ving after a night out
food blasts through
of our beleaguered
load is precisely the
following a few drinks
by a lake and reflect
magic mushrooms are
two we want bright
ersation, action and
romance and stolen
the culinary equi-
loud, and colorful.

CALCUTTA-STYLE
SIKH KEBAB ROLLS

—

FOR THE GARNISH: *½ onion, thinly sliced ~ 2 tbsp lime juice* **FOR THE MINT CHUTNEY:** *2 handfuls of cilantro leaves, finely chopped ~ handful of mint leaves, finely chopped ~ 1 tbsp finely grated ginger ~ 1 tbsp finely chopped garlic ~ 1 tsp chopped green chili ~ 2 tbsp desiccated coconut ~ good pinch of salt ~ 1 tbsp lime juice ~ ¼–⅓ cup water* **FOR THE KEBAB:** *½ lb ground lamb ~ 1 tbsp finely grated ginger ~ 2 cloves garlic, crushed or very finely chopped ~ ½ onion, very finely chopped ~ handful of mint leaves, finely chopped ~ handful of cilantro leaves, finely chopped ~ 1 green chili, deseeded and finely chopped ~ 1 tsp garam masala ~ ½ tsp chili powder ~ ½ tsp salt ~ 3½ tbsp melted butter, for basting* **TO SERVE:** *large circular pita breads* **YOU WILL NEED:** *4 skewers*

There are a number of restaurants around Calcutta's famous New Market like Nizam's and Badshah that serve a variety of tandoori meat dishes, including chicken kathi rolls and mutton rolls. When I was there for a week I got addicted to these places, loving the deep, rich meat flavor imparted by the tandoor alongside the fresh flavors of lime, onion, and chili that are wrapped up alongside them in a thin, fried paratha.

So, this is my take on a sikh kebab roll, with the addition of a mint chutney that is extremely simple to make.

Milton's Method 🖝 First prepare the garnish. Put the thinly sliced onion in a shallow bowl and marinate with the lime juice. Set aside while you prepare everything else.

Make the mint chutney by putting all the ingredients except the water into a blender (or use a pestle and mortar if you prefer), combining well, then adding enough water to create a thickish paste.

Put all the ingredients for the kebab, apart from the butter, into a large mixing bowl and mix together thoroughly with your hands.

Wet your hands (so that the mixture will not stick to them) and fashion fairly slender sausage shapes about 6 inches long around skewers. You should be able to make 4.

Preheat the broiler and place the skewers on a wire rack above a rimmed baking sheet. Brush the kebabs with melted butter and place under the broiler.

Turn every couple of minutes, basting as you go, until they are lightly browned on all sides and cooked all the way through. This should take about 12 minutes.

Brush one side of the pita breads with some of the melted butter and place under the broiler for a couple of minutes to warm up. Then turn over and warm the other side—you don't want to toast the pitas: they need to stay soft and pliable to wrap around your kebabs.

Serve each kebab on the buttered side of the pita, dribble over a generous helping of mint chutney, scatter a few slices of onion, and wrap into a roll. Eat straightaway.

CHICKEN TIKKA KEBABS

WITH KEBAB-SHOP SALAD

———

FOR THE KEBABS: *1 lb boneless skinless chicken breasts, cut into ¾–inch pieces ~ 2 tbsp lemon juice ~ 1 tsp salt ~ 3 tbsp Greek-style plain yogurt ~ 2 cloves garlic, crushed ~ 2 tsp finely grated ginger ~ ½ tsp smoked paprika ~ ½ tsp cayenne pepper ~ 1 tsp ground cumin ~ pinch of garam masala ~ 2 tbsp melted butter, for brushing* **FOR THE SALAD:** *¼ red cabbage, very thinly sliced ~ handful of lettuce, very thinly sliced ~ ½ red onion, halved and very thinly sliced ~ 1 carrot, peeled and finely grated ~ 2 pickled jalapeño peppers (1 per person), roughly chopped ~ ½ cucumber, halved lengthwise and thinly sliced ~ 1 large tomato, thinly sliced ~ juice of ½ lemon ~ glug of olive oil ~ handful of parsley, very finely chopped* **TO SERVE:** *warmed pita breads* **YOU WILL NEED:** *4 skewers*

The kebab is the quintessential accompaniment to a drunken night, and the chicken tikka kebab is a personal favorite of mine. Ideally, you should already have the chicken marinating for at least a few hours before you cook, so you could think about doing this before you start drinking so that it (a) tastes better and (b) is really simple to prepare. However, if time is at a premium, the recipe still works with a modest marinating time.

The salad is more Turkish than Indian in origin, I suppose, and this recipe is designed to emulate the typical British kebab-shop salad, with a couple of embellishments. The trick is to make sure that all the ingredients are cut really finely to get that authentic crispy texture.

Milton's Method ☞ Put the chicken pieces in a bowl with the lemon juice and salt. Stir or use your hands to make sure all the chicken pieces are well coated. Leave to marinate for 10–15 minutes then add the yogurt, garlic, ginger, paprika, cayenne pepper, ground cumin, and garam masala. Cover and marinate in the fridge for as long as possible (up to 24 hours). If time is short, then simply pop it in the fridge while you prepare the salad. To make the salad, just throw all the ingredients in a bowl together and mix well.

To cook the chicken, preheat your broiler. While it's heating up, place the chicken pieces on the skewers and brush with the melted butter. Place the skewers on a grill pan, under the broiler, and cook so that the edges get a little charred but the overall effect is lightly browned. This should take 12–15 minutes in total, turning 2 to 3 times.

Serve with the salad and warmed pita breads.

HENRY AND LISA'S MONTSERRAT-STYLE CHICKEN WINGS

—

1 lb chicken wings ~ 1 lemon ~ 5 tsp all-purpose seasoning, sometimes called "season-all" ~ 1 tsp paprika ~ 2 tsp allspice (ground pimento) ~ salt and pepper ~ 3 cloves garlic, finely chopped ~ 1 large tomato, roughly chopped ~ ½ tbsp fresh thyme or a bit less dry thyme ~ good splash of Worcestershire sauce ~ 1½ capfuls malt vinegar ~ 1 chili, chopped, according to taste ~ small drizzle of olive oil ~ small squeeze of ketchup **TO SERVE:** *rice and salad*

Henry and Lisa are two of my friends from north London who are used to late nights, serious cooking, and waiting for the birds to start singing. Unless they're chickens, that is. In which case, they'll probably already be in Henry and Lisa's oven. Henry's chicken wing recipe has been handed down from his mother, who was born in Montserrat.

Milton's Method ☞ Preheat your oven to 375°F. Clean the wings with cut segments of lemon, remove any stray feathers, and place the wings on a baking sheet. Sprinkle the all-purpose seasoning, paprika, allspice, and a little salt and pepper over the wings.

Use your hands to rub the seasoning thoroughly onto the wings, then add the rest of the ingredients and massage them in well. Cover the baking sheet with foil and bake in the oven for 35 minutes.

Remove the foil and bake for a further 35–40 minutes, taking the tray out a couple of times to give the wings a good shoggling (shaking) so they don't stick to the tray. As they bake, the liquid will evaporate and the wings will develop a rich color and a delicious crispness.

Serve the wings on their own, or with rice and salad.

"During one of my treks through Afghanistan, we lost our corkscrew. We were compelled to live on food and water for several days."

W.C. Fields

PAKISTANI LAMB KOFTA

—

 (fussy)

FOR THE KOFTA: *¾ lb ground lamb ~ 1 tsp peeled and finely grated ginger ~ ½ small onion, finely chopped ~ 2 green chilis, finely chopped ~ 2 cloves garlic, peeled and finely chopped ~ 1 egg ~ 2 tbsp gram flour (or all-purpose flour) ~ ½ tsp salt ~ ½ tsp garam masala ~ handful of cilantro leaves and stalks, finely chopped* **FOR THE SAUCE:** *vegetable or peanut oil ~ 1 onion, finely chopped ~ 1 bay leaf ~ 1 small stick cinnamon ~ 1 tbsp peeled and finely grated ginger ~ 2 cloves garlic, crushed ~ ½ tsp ground turmeric ~ ½ tsp cayenne pepper ~ 1 cup canned diced tomatoes ~ salt and pepper ~ 2¼ cups water* **TO SERVE:** *wide rice noodles ~ handful of cilantro leaves, roughly chopped, to garnish*

Pakistani and Bangladeshi meat dishes have been staples of mine ever since a visit to the legendary Tayyabs restaurant on Fieldgate Street in Whitechapel (where Stalin once lived and where Big Ben—the bell—was made).

I prefer eating this best with wide rice noodles, and thinking of it as an Asian version of fettuccine with meatballs.

Milton's Method ☞ Combine all the ingredients for the kofta in a large bowl and mix well with your hands. Wet your hands and make individual balls about the size of small plums. Put these on a plate and set aside while you make the sauce.

Heat some vegetable or peanut oil in a large nonstick saucepan and add the onion, bay leaf, and cinnamon. Cook on medium-high heat until the onion is golden.

Add the ginger and garlic, stir and cook for a minute, add the spices, stir and cook for 10 seconds, then add the tomatoes and seasoning.

Cook for about 5 minutes to allow some of the liquid to evaporate, stirring occasionally. Add the water, bring to a boil, and simmer for a few minutes to reduce again, then gently add the meatballs to the sauce. Cover the pan, place on low heat, and leave to simmer for 15–20 minutes. Remove the cinnamon and bay leaf.

Serve with wide rice noodles tossed in butter and garnish with chopped cilantro leaves.

CHAR-GRILLED VEGETABLE AND CHEESE QUESADILLA

WITH FRIED EGG

———

1 tbsp olive oil ~ ½ tsp salt ~ 1 red bell pepper, deseeded and thinly sliced ~ 8 cherry tomatoes ~ 4 corn tortillas ~ 6 oz aged cheddar, grated ~ 4 scallions, very finely shredded ~ 1 jalapeño pepper, finely chopped ~ 1 tsp dried oregano ~ black pepper ~ 2 free-range eggs ~ olive oil, for frying **TO SERVE:** *lime wedges ~ chipotle sauce ~ Greek yogurt or sour cream*

The first time I tried this recipe I used eggs bought at the roadside from a house in the middle of nowhere. When I opened the box, I discovered beautiful pastel-blue eggs, marked with their laid-on date in a neat, penciled hand. Cracking the thin blue shells revealed boisterous, large orange yolks that made the best fried eggs I had ever tasted. Even more delicious when placed on a quesadilla filled with cheese and tomatoes and peppers that have been deliberately slightly burnt a little to give them a smoky flavor. You can use oil to fry your quesadilla, but I prefer to dry fry mine—this recipe has plenty of fat going on already.

Milton's Method ☞ Preheat the broiler. Pour the olive oil and salt into a small bowl and add the bell pepper and tomatoes. Mix to cover well with oil then place them on a baking sheet under the broiler, fairly close to the heat. You want the skins to blacken a little—there's plenty of juice so they won't burn to a crisp too easily. Once you've got the smell of a little smoke, turn everything over and cook the other side—this should take 5–6 minutes.

Place one tortilla in a frying pan of the same size. Evenly spread on half of the cheese, scallions, tomatoes, bell pepper, jalapeño, and oregano and season with black pepper.

Place another tortilla on top and gently press it down. Cook on medium-high heat until the bottom tortilla has become toasted and golden (2–3 minutes), then place a plate over the top of the frying pan, flip the quesadilla out onto the plate, and return to the pan to cook the other side, again for 2–3 minutes.

Repeat (for the second quesadilla), set aside, and fry your eggs. I prefer to do this in olive oil over low to medium heat so that the white stays soft. Cut the quesadillas into triangles and serve each with an egg on top, a squeeze of lime, plenty of chipotle sauce, possibly some Greek yogurt or sour cream, and definitely a cold beer.

QUICK COUSCOUS
CHICKEN BIRYANI

---

2 skinless boneless chicken breasts and thighs, cut into ¾-inch chunks ~ 1 tsp cayenne pepper ~ 1 tsp red paprika ~ ½ tsp turmeric ~ 2 tsp ground coriander ~ 1 tsp curry powder ~ salt ~ ½ tsp garlic powder ~ 2 cups chicken stock ~ large pinch of saffron ~ 2 tbsp butter ~ 1 tbsp vegetable oil ~ 2 onions, thinly sliced into half rings ~ 2 bay leaves ~ 4 whole cloves ~ 1 small stick of cinnamon ~ 3 cardamom pods ~ 1 cup couscous ~ ½ pound potatoes, cut into 1-inch chunks and boiled until just cooked ~ ½ cup frozen peas **TO SERVE:** *cucumber raita ~ papadums*

In Karnataka, and Kerala in particular (the best was in Kannur, Kerala), I ate biryani all the time, most often goat biryani that I quickly learnt to eat with my right hand off large banana leaves. Crisp papadums are served with the meal and provide a great textural contrast. The tender meat and fragrant rice are wonderful, but biryani is something that generally takes a long time to cook. I decided to create a shorter, easier version.

It does not pretend to be comparable to a "proper" biryani, and purists will certainly scoff, but it is extraordinarily quick and easy to prepare and is still very tasty.

Milton's Method Place the chicken pieces in a large bowl and add the cayenne pepper, paprika, turmeric, coriander, curry powder, 1 tsp salt, and garlic powder. Make sure each piece of chicken is well coated with the spice mix. Heat your stock (or make it up, if you're using a bouillon cube), and add the saffron. Leave to stand.

In a heavy frying pan, heat the butter and oil over medium-high heat. There is quite a lot of fat, but this is important to keep the chicken tender and the couscous buttery. Once the butter has melted and is bubbling a little, add the chicken pieces and cook until colored slightly on all sides. They should not be cooked through. This will take just 3–4 minutes. Using a slotted spoon, remove the chicken pieces and set aside.

Using the same fat and the same pan, add the onions, bay leaves, cloves, cinnamon, cardamom, and a good pinch of salt and cook the onions for around 12 minutes, stirring regularly until the onions are richly colored but not burnt.

Add the dried couscous, stir, then add the chicken, boiled potato pieces, and frozen peas. Finally, add the stock, stir well, cover, and turn the heat down to very low. Keep on the heat for 5 minutes then kill the flame completely but leave the lid on for a further 10 minutes to allow the flavors to infuse and the chicken to cook through. Remove the bay leaves, cinnamon stick, and cardamom pods.

Serve immediately with cucumber raita and as many papadums as you can get your hands on.

WELL-
OILED

—

Fried food is just as ubiqu
hedonistic night as losing cas
waking up in the morning wit
But frying can be dangerous.
serve as a cautionary tale. Aft
going home and cooking som
an area of London where Tur
of fruit, vegetables, and chest
picked up my nuts and headed
In my drunken wisdom I decic
whacked the heat on high, p
got a beer, and went and sat
think about the wok or the ch
sounded like small-arms fire c
the sound of chestnuts explc
the kitchen walls. There is so
the unctuousness that fryir
evenly across the palate. Jus

us an accompaniment to a
own the back of taxi seats or
our shoes and socks still on.
e of my frying stories should
a night out, at 4 a.m. I fancied
hestnuts. I lived at the time in
h grocers sell a fantastic array
ts, twenty-four hours a day. I
me. Would I roast them? No.
to fry them in oil in a wok. I
in the oil and the chestnuts,
the living room and did not
tnuts again until I heard what
ing from the kitchen. It was
ng and spattering oil all over
thing deeply satisfying about
imparts, with flavor spread
on't kill yourself doing it.

BACKHENDL (AUSTRIAN FRIED CHICKEN)

WITH STYRIAN POTATO SALAD

———

FOR THE POTATO SALAD: *1 lb waxy potatoes ~ ½ cup vegetable stock, home-made or store-bought ~ ¼ cup pumpkin seed oil (or extra virgin olive oil) ~ ¼ cup cider vinegar ~ 1 onion, finely diced ~ salt and pepper ~ 2 tbsp pumpkin seeds ~ handful of chives, finely chopped* **FOR THE CHICKEN:** *2 chicken breasts, 2 drumsticks, and 2 thighs, skin removed ~ 1 cup flour ~ 1 tsp onion powder ~ 1 tsp garlic powder ~ 2 tsp salt ~ 1 tsp pepper ~ 3 eggs ~ 1 cup fine bread crumbs ~ vegetable oil, for frying*

According to my Austrian friends, there are only two KFCs in the whole of Austria—both in Vienna. This dish probably explains why. It is fried chicken, Austrian style, and in Austria it is usually served with a potato salad.

My difficulty with this recipe is that the chicken should be deep-fried but, in an effort to spare you, my dear readers, from an ignominious end, here I have decided to shallow-fry and then bake the chicken, which I think gives equally good results.

Delicious pumpkin seed oil is a common, though still expensive, commodity in Austria. If you cannot find it, try using good-quality olive oil instead.

Milton's Method ☞ Put the potatoes, whole and with their skins, into a large saucepan of cold water. Bring to a boil and cook for around 20 minutes, until cooked through but not mushy. Drain and set aside to cool a little.

To make the dressing, mix the vegetable stock, pumpkin seed oil, cider vinegar, onion, and salt and pepper to taste in a small bowl. Stir well.

Peel and slice the potatoes and place in a large bowl then pour the dressing over them. Set aside to allow the potatoes to absorb the dressing. Toast the pumpkin seeds and add them as garnish along with the chopped chives.

To cook the chicken, preheat the oven to 350°F. In a large bowl, add the flour, onion powder, garlic powder, salt, and pepper and mix well to combine. Beat the eggs in a shallow bowl and place the bread crumbs in another. Coat the chicken pieces in the flour, then dip them in the egg, and finally in the bread crumbs. Make sure each piece is well coated. Put on a plate, ready to cook.

Place a large heavy frying pan over medium heat and add vegetable oil to about a ½-inch depth. Once the oil is hot, place the chicken pieces in the pan. Be careful of spitting oil. Cook on each side until the bread crumbs are crisp and golden (7–8 minutes) then drain and place on a baking sheet lined with foil. Place in the oven for 15–20 minutes or until the chicken is cooked through.

Serve with the potato salad.

FRIED BROCCOLI

WITH ANCHOVIES, GARLIC,
CHILI, AND CAPERS

---

*1 tbsp peanut or vegetable oil ~ 12 canned anchovy fillets, finely chopped ~
2 cloves garlic, finely chopped ~ 2 red chilis, thinly sliced ~ 1 large head of broccoli,
washed and cut into small florets ~ 1 tbsp capers ~ 2 tbsp pumpkin seeds*

You can eat this as a side dish or combine it with some pasta and
some torn buffalo mozzarella to make a more substantial meal.
The anchovies and capers provide all the salt you need—don't add
any more.

Milton's Method ☞ In a large frying pan or wok, heat the oil over
high heat and add the anchovies, garlic, and chilis. Cook for about
2 minutes, stirring constantly and crushing the anchovies with the
back of your spoon. Make sure the garlic does not burn.

Add the broccoli and the capers, stir well, and cook for about
5 minutes, until the broccoli has colored slightly but is still firm and
crunchy. In a separate pan, dry-toast the
pumpkin seeds until they are light brown
and crunchy.

Serve the broccoli sprinkled with
the pumpkin seeds.

"Never despise a drink
because it is easy
to make and/or uses
commercial mixes.
Unquestioning devotion
to authenticity is,
in any department of
life, a mark of the
naive—or worse."

Kingsley Amis

PORK SCHNITZEL SANDWICH

WITH CHEESE AND CHILI
AND A WATERCRESS SALAD

———

2 pork loin steaks, each about 6 oz ~ 1 cup all-purpose flour ~ salt and pepper ~ 3 oz finely grated Parmesan ~ handful of thyme, finely chopped ~ 1 tsp chili flakes ~ 1 cup fine white bread crumbs ~ 2 eggs, beaten ~ vegetable oil, for frying **TO SERVE:** *2 white crusty rolls (such as Kaiser rolls) ~ 2 cups watercress ~ 1 tbsp lemon juice ~ 1 tbsp olive oil*

The Austrians have much to teach the rest of the world on the subject of drinking and the food required to accompany it. Believe me: I know. During one debauched evening at a southern Austrian *Buschenschank*—a kind of rural wine tavern where the wine is produced at the tavern's own vineyard and food is sourced locally— we were served roughly six bottles of wine per person and a meaty banquet that included rye bread with warm beef dripping, pork dripping, roast pork, various charcuterie, chicken liver pâté, sheep's-milk cheese, and slices of beef in jelly with garnishes and condiments including gherkins, grated horseradish, and mustard.

This dish takes its inspiration from the Austrian countryside with a nod to Vienna and the *Schnitzelsemmel*—a sandwich whose primary ingredient is one of Austria's most famous exports: the schnitzel, sometimes made from veal, but often from pork as well. In Austria, this is usually made with a Kaiser roll, but any kind of white crusty roll will do.

Milton's Method Flatten the steaks between 2 pieces of plastic wrap with a rolling pin, so that they're about ⅛ inch thick.

Season the flour generously with salt and pepper in a shallow bowl. Combine the Parmesan, chopped thyme, chili flakes, and bread crumbs and place in a separate shallow bowl.

Coat the pork with the flour, then dredge through the beaten egg and cover in the bread crumb mix. Make sure that the meat is evenly and generously coated. Repeat with the other steak. Ideally, leave in the fridge for at least 10 minutes to let the bread crumbs stick. Shallow-fry in a little vegetable oil on medium-high heat until both sides are crisp and golden, 5–7 minutes per side.

Serve in the rolls with the watercress drizzled with the lemon juice and a little olive oil.

SPANISH-STYLE FRIED GARLIC-PRAWN BAGUETTE

—

2 large tomatoes, finely diced ~ ⅓ cup good-quality extra virgin olive oil ~ 4 large cloves garlic, crushed and very finely chopped ~ salt and pepper ~ 2 tsp crushed red pepper ~ 8 very large prawns, uncooked, with shells (4 per person) ~ 1 tsp sweet paprika ~ ¼ cup brandy ~ 1 lemon (½ juiced, ½ cut into 2 wedges) ~ handful of parsley, finely chopped ~ 1 fresh white baguette

Ah, those many hours I have whiled away drinking sherry and cava and eating garlicky prawns, patatas bravas, tortilla Española, and the like, have been some of the happiest of my life. This is an extremely quick and simple recipe to prepare and perfect for a summer drinking snack with cold beer or a fresh white wine.

Milton's Method ☞ First make the tomato salsa. In a small bowl, add the tomatoes, a glug of the olive oil, and one of the cloves of garlic and season generously with salt, pepper, and a pinch of crushed red pepper. Mix thoroughly and set aside to allow the flavors to mingle.

Warm the remaining olive oil in a frying pan over medium-high heat, then add the rest of the garlic and cook for about 30 seconds. Be careful not to burn it. Add the prawns, the remaining crushed red pepper, and the sweet paprika. Stir. The prawns should be pinkening already. Add the brandy (careful—there may be a quick burst of flame) and then the lemon juice. Add the chopped parsley and a little salt, swirl the pan, and, when they're pink on the bottom, flip the prawns over to cook the other side. They should need no more than about 4 minutes in total. When the prawns are pink all over, remove them from the pan and set them aside. Take the pan off the heat and reserve the cooking sauce.

Divide the baguette between 2 plates and slice lengthwise, peel the prawns, and place in the baguette halves. This is a messy business that you can make the most of by licking your fingers frequently. Spoon some of the cooking liquor over them, then the tomato salsa, and finish with a squeeze of lemon. Garnish with the lemon wedges.

Tuck in.

THE FRIED
MUSHROOM BURGER

—

½ cup all-purpose flour ~ 1 tsp salt ~ pepper ~ handful of finely chopped chives ~ 2 portobello mushroom caps (1 per person), 2 parasol caps (1 per person), or 4 (¾-inch-thick) slices of giant puffball (2 per person) ~ 4 slices bacon **FOR THE VINAIGRETTE:** *1 tsp Dijon mustard ~ ½ clove garlic, minced ~ 1 tbsp white wine vinegar ~ 4 tbsp olive oil ~ salt and pepper, to taste* **TO SERVE:** *2 soft white buns ~ handful of salad leaves*

There are a few different options with this mushroom burger, but of varying degrees of practicality. The easiest type of mushroom to get hold of is a portobello (readily available in most greengrocers and supermarkets), but it's worth trying this recipe with a couple of more exotic types of fungi. The tastiest is the parasol; the most fun is the giant puffball. All three are large mushrooms, and all you will need to do is to cook 1 or 2 pieces per person to rustle up a satisfying meal.

If you'd prefer to keep it vegetarian, dispense with the bacon and add a little more fat to your pan.

If you are picking wild mushrooms, make sure you know what you're doing—some types of mushroom can be lethal. But the giant puffball is one that you cannot mistake—if you see something the size and shape of a soccer ball and it's not a soccer ball, then it's probably a giant puffball.

Milton's Method ☞ Season the flour with the salt, a few grinds of black pepper, and the finely chopped chives.

Dampen each piece of mushroom very slightly with some water and dip in the flour so that it is thinly coated all over.

Combine all the ingredients for the vinaigrette. Add a little oil to a heavy frying pan and heat over medium heat. Add the bacon and cook until crisp. Remove the bacon and keep warm.

Add the floured mushrooms to the pan and cook, turning once, until the mushrooms are crispy and golden on the outside. This should take a matter of minutes. Place the mushrooms in the soft buns with the bacon. Add salad leaves on top and spoon a generous amount of dressing over the top.

Eat immediately.

SPICY SMOKED TOFU BURGERS

WITH CORIANDER, ROAST
SQUASH, AND AVOCADO PURÉE

   (toil)

FOR THE TOFU BURGERS: *1 onion, roughly chopped ~ 1 clove garlic, chopped ~ 1 chili, chopped ~ 1 medium carrot, peeled and finely grated ~ 1 cup canned red kidney beans ~ 6 oz firm smoked tofu, drained ~ 1 tsp sweet paprika ~ 1 tsp ground coriander ~ 1 tbsp sesame seeds ~ handful of flat-leaf parsley, finely chopped ~ 2 tsp vegetable stock powder ~ 2 tsp cornstarch ~ 1 egg, beaten* **FOR THE CORIANDER ROAST SQUASH:** *1 butternut squash, peeled and roughly chopped ~ 2 tbsp olive oil ~ 1 tbsp lightly crushed coriander seeds ~ 2 cloves garlic, crushed ~ 2 dried bird's-eye chilis, crushed ~ ½ tsp salt ~ pepper* **FOR THE AVOCADO PURÉE:** *2 ripe avocados ~ 2 scallions, finely chopped ~ good pinch of sea salt ~ glug of extra virgin olive oil ~ 2 tbsp water* **TO SERVE:** *burger buns*

You may (or may not) think of tofu as a dreary, insipid abomination that only has relevance if you are interested in saving the rainforests and hundreds of thousands of cattle from being slaughtered in hideously inhumane ways. And these are both laudable aims that I think are well worth pursuing. But for the skeptical amongst you, I'd also like to urge you to rethink your dislike of this much-maligned product by trying this recipe that is quite expressly a "tofu dish for people who don't like tofu."

Smoked tofu is available in many different flavors and strengths; the strongest can be extremely intense—salty, dense, and smoky, with a consistency like a semi-hard cheese. The most important thing is to make sure that the tofu is firm, as a too-soggy tofu will result in sad and sloppy burgers.

This can be a vegan recipe if you exclude the egg, but including it will help your burgers to bind together more effectively.

Milton's Method ☞ Preheat your oven to 425°F. Line a baking sheet with parchment paper. Whack all the burger ingredients in a food processor and blitz for a few seconds to form a rough paste; it's good to retain a bit of texture. If you don't have a food processor, use a potato masher to get the consistency right.

Form the mixture into 4 burgers with wet hands and place on the baking sheet. At the same time, prepare the squash by mixing it with all the other ingredients and placing in the oven on a baking sheet.

Bake the burgers for 35–40 minutes until light golden brown. The squash should take the same amount of time. While the burgers and squash are in the oven, make the avocado purée by mashing the avocado flesh with the back of a fork then combining with the other ingredients to make a creamy purée.

Remove the burgers from the oven and leave to rest for a couple of minutes. This will help them to set.

Serve in buns, or on their own, with the purée and squash.

SLOSHED
STARCH

—

Alcohol may be calorific
200 calories in a pint of
wine), but drinking none
evenhungrier.You'll quite
you can get your hands
vigorous night of partyin
partying. The best way to
give you the kind of pur
going through the night
am a big lover of starchy
they have recently receiv
media. Without pasta, br
I don't know how I would
Well, I guess I'd still h
Now, if I didn't have tho

there are approximately
er or a medium glass of
eless tends to make us
ely need all the calories
if you're planning on a
nd possibly even after-
oak up the booze, and to
seful energy to keep you
to eat carbohydrates. I
rbs, despite the bad press
from the protein-loving
d, potatoes, and noodles,
ake it through the week.
e fine wine and cheese.
I really would struggle.

AUTHENTIC
SMOKY CHICKEN
BURRITO
—

4 boneless skinless chicken breasts **FOR THE MARINADE:** *4 cloves garlic, peeled and roughly chopped ~ 1 red onion, peeled and roughly chopped ~ 2 regular green chilis, chopped ~ 2 tsp cumin ~ 2 tsp dried oregano ~ 1 tbsp lime juice ~ 1 tsp sugar ~ 2 tsp salt ~ pepper* **FOR THE RICE:** *½ cup long-grain rice ~ large handful of cilantro, chopped ~ juice of 1 lime ~ ½ tsp salt* **FOR THE BEANS:** *1 tbsp olive oil ~ 1 small onion, chopped ~ 1 clove garlic, crushed and finely chopped ~ 1 canned chipotle pepper (soft), chopped ~ 1 tsp cumin ~ 1 cup canned pinto beans, rinsed and drained ~ ½ cup chicken stock ~ 1 tsp cornstarch ~ salt and pepper* **TO SERVE:** *flour tortillas ~ red chili sauce ~ grated cheddar cheese ~ sour cream*

The chicken really does need time to marinate for this recipe, and it's best if you prepare it the night before to cook the following evening. This is a meal in itself and needs no accompaniment but a cold beer. The great chicken flavor is mainly due to the chipotle marinade and the Maillard reaction that you get from cooking.

Milton's Method ☞ For the marinade, combine all the ingredients in a blender, and blitz. Prick the chicken pieces with a sharp knife and place in an airtight container or sealable sandwich bag with the marinade. Leave to marinate in the fridge for 12–24 hours.

Prepare the rice by following the package instructions. When the rice is cooked, add the cilantro, lime juice, and salt. Set aside and keep warm.

For the beans, heat the olive oil in a nonstick saucepan over medium heat and add the onion. Cook, stirring occasionally, until softened, then add the garlic, chipotle pepper, and cumin. Cook for

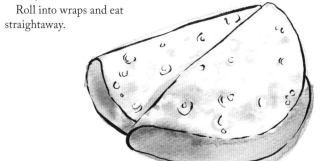

a further minute or two then add the beans and the stock and season well. Bring to a boil and simmer for 5 minutes. Mix the cornstarch with a little water and add to the pan. Stir until the sauce has thickened a little and become slightly glutinous. Set aside and keep warm.

To cook the chicken, heat a heavy griddle pan or a George Foreman Grill to high then add the chicken, pressing it down to sear and caramelize the surface. Once the chicken has pronounced sear marks on one side, turn to cook the other side. This should take about 8–10 minutes in total. Turn off the heat and leave the chicken to rest and cook through in the pan for 2–3 minutes.

Heat the tortillas, following the package instructions, and add a generous serving of rice and beans to the middle of each. Cut the chicken into ¾-inch cubes and place on top, and add chili sauce, cheese, and sour cream to taste.

Roll into wraps and eat straightaway.

FETTUCCINE WITH MEATBALLS AND CHEESE

—

FOR THE MEATBALLS: *½ lb ground beef ~ ¼ lb bulk pork sausage ~ 2 cloves garlic, finely chopped ~ 1 egg ~ 1 tbsp grated Parmesan ~ 2 tbsp bread crumbs ~ 1 tbsp dried oregano ~ handful of parsley, finely chopped ~ salt and pepper, to taste* **FOR THE TOMATO SAUCE:** *2 tbsp olive oil ~ ½ onion, very finely chopped ~ 2 cloves garlic, crushed or finely chopped ~ 1 red chili, deseeded and finely chopped ~ ½ tsp chili flakes ~ 1 tbsp dried oregano ~ ⅓ cup red wine ~ 1 tbsp balsamic vinegar ~ 1 14.5 oz can diced tomatoes ~ ½ tsp sugar ~ grated zest of ½ lemon ~ ½ cup water ~ salt and pepper, to taste* **TO SERVE:** *½ lb dried fettuccine ~ 3 oz grated Parmesan*

Okay, so cooking meatballs is a mainstay of gangster films; but put away the attitude and the razor blades for slicing the garlic. Right now. Who do you think you are? Some kind of wiseguy?

Fine. Let's begin. Are we making our own pasta here? Of course we're not. Who do you think I am? Jamie frickin' Oliver? Antonio bleedin' Carluccio? No. Go to the shop to buy your pasta. Fettuccine is best with meatballs. All you have to do is make the meatballs, cook a simple tomato sauce, and grate a bunch of cheese on top. *Semplice!* (Simple) *Perfetto!* (Perfect).

Milton's Method ☞ Combine all the ingredients for the meatballs in a large bowl and mix well—use a spoon if you prefer, but hands are best. With wet hands, divide the mixture up into small balls the size of walnuts—you should end up with about a dozen. Put them on a plate, cover with some plastic wrap, and place in the fridge until needed.

For the sauce, put a frying pan on medium heat, add the olive oil, and fry the onion for 5–6 minutes, stirring frequently, until softened and just beginning to turn gold. Add the garlic, red chili, chili flakes, and oregano, cook for about a minute, then add the wine. Be careful—the pan will spit.

Turn up the heat, bring to a boil, and reduce the liquid by half, stirring, then add the balsamic vinegar. Simmer for another couple of minutes then add the canned tomatoes, sugar, lemon zest, and water. Season generously. Stir well, bring to a boil, and simmer over low heat for 10 minutes.

Place the meatballs in the tomato sauce and cook on low heat for 15–20 minutes, turning occasionally so that they get cooked through. Cook the fettuccine according to the package instructions.

Serve the meatballs in their sauce with the fettuccine and a generous grating of Parmesan.

HOMEMADE
POTATO GNOCCHI

WITH A RICH RAGÙ

———

FOR THE RAGÙ *3 tbsp olive oil ~ 1 red onion, diced ~ 2 stalks celery, diced ~ 1 carrot, diced ~ 2 bay leaves ~ ¼ lb bacon, roughly chopped ~ ½ lb ground beef ~ 3½ oz chicken livers, trimmed, washed, and finely chopped ~ 1 cup red wine ~ 1 14.5-oz can diced tomatoes ~ 3 tbsp tomato purée ~ 1 tsp grated nutmeg ~ salt and pepper* **FOR THE GNOCCHI:** *1½ cups cold mashed potatoes ~ 2 cups flour (and extra for dusting) ~ 1 egg, beaten ~ salt and pepper*

One of my Italian friends tells the story of how, as a child, when she used to get out of bed in the morning and go down to the kitchen, her mother would already be cooking the ragù for the evening meal. As it was bubbling away, her mother would poach an egg or two in the sauce and serve it with some bread for breakfast and carry on cooking.

While most of the recipes I have included in this cookbook have been designed with instant gratification in mind, this is one best suited to a Sunday afternoon, perhaps, where it would be wise to sit back and open a bottle or two of red and wait for your ragù to simmer, mature, and thicken.

Milton's Method ☞ In a large, heavy Dutch oven, heat the olive oil over medium heat and add the onion, celery, carrot, and bay leaves. Cook for about 10 minutes, stirring now and again, then add the bacon. Turn the heat up and allow the bacon to color slightly before adding the beef and the chicken livers. Once all the meat is well browned, add the wine, tomatoes, tomato purée, nutmeg, and salt and pepper. Stir well, bring to a boil, and turn the heat down to low. Simmer for 2 hours, stirring occasionally to stop the sauce from sticking. Add a little water if it does. Remove the bay leaves.

To prepare the gnocchi, combine the mashed potatoes, flour, and beaten egg, along with some salt and pepper, in a large bowl and knead together to make a dough. Roll this into a ball, then take chunks from the bowl and roll them, with a little extra flour to prevent sticking, into long worms about ¼ inch thick. Cut into ½-inch lengths and place on a plate dusted with a little more flour.

When the ragù is ready, bring a large pan of salted water to a boil and drop in the gnocchi. Once they bob to the top, after 3–4 minutes, they are ready. Remove from the pan with a slotted spoon.

Serve immediately with a generous helping of ragù.

MILTON'S BAGUETTE, BUTTER, AND PLUM JAM PUDDING

—

3½ tbsp butter (and extra for greasing) ~ 5 tbsp plum jam ~ 1 slightly stale baguette, thinly sliced ~ ⅓ cup golden raisins ~ 2 large eggs ~ 2 large egg yolks ~ ¼ cup granulated sugar ~ 1 vanilla pod, halved ~ 1⅓ cups heavy cream ~ 1⅓ cups whole milk ~ ⅓ cup French brandy ~ 2 tbsp soft brown sugar
TO SERVE: *cream or vanilla ice cream*

This gloriously indulgent pudding is packed full of calorific treats (like most of the best desserts are).

Milton's Method ☞ Preheat your oven to 350°F. Grease a small, shallow, rectangular baking dish. Spread butter and some of the jam on both sides of your sliced baguette and place the baguette slices in overlapping layers in the dish, adding the raisins as you go.

Make a basic custard by beating the eggs, egg yolks, and granulated sugar in a mixing bowl until they are creamy, then scrape the seeds from the vanilla pod into the mixture. Beat in the cream, milk, and brandy. Pour the mixture over the bread slices in the baking dish and leave for 20 minutes so the bread can soak it all up. Sprinkle the soft brown sugar on top.

Place the baking dish in a roasting pan and pour boiling water around the outside—you are basically creating a bain-marie-type arrangement so that the pudding poaches rather than roasts. Place in the oven and bake for about 45 minutes until golden on top.

Remove from the oven and leave to rest for 10 minutes. While it's resting, glaze the top with the remaining plum jam, loosened with a couple of teaspoons of hot water.

Serve with fresh cream or vanilla ice cream.

"I don't believe in dining on an empty stomach."

W.C. Fields

PAD MILTON

—

6 oz dried ho fun rice noodles ~ 4 oz firm tofu, cut into ¾ x ½-inch strips ~ 2–3 tbsp vegetable or peanut oil ~ 4 scallions, finely shredded, dividing the white and green parts ~ 3 cloves garlic, crushed ~ ½ lb uncooked, shelled, and deveined large prawns ~ 2 eggs, beaten ~ 2 oz bean sprouts ~ 3 tbsp fish sauce (nam pla) ~ 2 tbsp lime juice ~ 1 tbsp soft brown sugar ~ 2 tbsp tamarind paste ~ ½ tsp dried hot chili flakes ~ ground white pepper **TO SERVE:** *2 tbsp freshly toasted and lightly crushed peanuts ~ lime wedges*

This is my take on the classic pad Thai. The secret is in getting the balance right between sweet (from the sugar), sour (from the lime juice and tamarind), salty (from the fish sauce), and spicy (from the chili). Of all the pad Thai dishes I ever ate in Thailand, only one really disappointed. It was made with stringy, instant-style noodles. It's important to use dried rice noodles, and I prefer the wide, "ho-fun" style. Don't be put off by the long list of ingredients— the only effort required is in taking them out of the cupboard as the cooking itself is a cinch and so quick.

Milton's Method ☞ Soak the noodles in hot water, following the package instructions. Pat the tofu dry with paper towels. Heat a wok over high heat and add 2 tablespoons oil. Stir-fry the tofu until it starts to brown, then add the white part of the scallions and the garlic and continue to stir-fry.

Meanwhile, when the noodles are softened but still have a little firmness, drain them and, while they are still in the colander, pour a little oil over them and run your fingers through the noodles with the oil to stop them from sticking together.

Add the prawns to the wok, cook until just pinkening slightly, then add the noodles and stir well.

Move the noodles and prawns to one side of the wok and add the beaten eggs to the other. Cook without stirring until the egg is loosely set—30 seconds or so—then break up and mix well with the noodles. Then in succession add the bean sprouts, green part of the scallions, fish sauce, lime juice, brown sugar, tamarind paste, and chili flakes, stirring and tossing the contents of the wok until well combined and the noodles are tender. Season with white pepper.

Serve immediately with peanuts scattered over each serving and a wedge of lime on the side.

TWICE-BAKED POTATOES

WITH CURRY PASTE,
CHEESE, AND PEAS

———

2 large baking potatoes ~ 1 onion, halved and thinly sliced ~ 1 tbsp olive oil ~ 3½ tbsp butter ~ 6 oz aged cheddar, grated ~ 2 tbsp Patak's balti curry paste ~ ½ cup frozen peas ~ 1 tbsp lemon juice ~ salt and pepper, to taste ~ handful of finely chopped chives **TO SERVE:** *1 red chili, finely sliced ~ Greek yogurt ~ green salad*

This is an old classic of mine that is surprisingly delicious and could not be easier to make. The one downside is that you'll have to wait for your potatoes to bake. You can, of course, take a shortcut by using the microwave, but you won't get the great flavor from the skin that baking in the oven gives.

Milton's Method ☞ Preheat your oven to 425°F. Bake the potatoes. I normally do this by pricking the potatoes with a fork a few times and putting them straight into the oven. No oil. No salt. No nuffink. They should take 45–60 minutes to cook. While the potatoes are cooking, fry the sliced onion in the olive oil over medium-high heat until it has taken on a little color. Set aside.

You want the skin of your potatoes crispy and the flesh soft and fluffy. Check by running a skewer through the potato. If it runs through cleanly then it's done.

Take the potatoes out and cut in half length-wise. Scoop the soft flesh into a large bowl and add the butter, cheese, fried onions, curry paste, frozen peas, lemon juice, salt and pepper, and half of the chives. Mix well then cram back into the potato shells. Return to the oven on a baking sheet, and bake for another 15 minutes until crispy on top.

Serve with some red chili and chives sprinkled on top, some Greek yogurt alongside, and a crisp green salad.

PLASTERED
PARTY
FOOD

—

Eating and drinking with frie
sures, but cooking for them
often isn't. People say that th
people hang out at parties, b
this maxim, the higher the
overall "good people quotier
sure I want people around me w
dish. For me it's a matter of
on producing food, it is har
Not everyone is the same—t
one knows at least one), for
something together while im
their sharp wit, amazing s
annoying superhuman-ness,
same way that I do. This ch
for dishes that are quick an
also fun and delicious to
human (perhaps), while also

s is one of life's great plea-
ile trying to have a good time
itchen is where all the best
the more people that know
kelihood that the kitchen's
will be reduced. And I'm not
n I'm still trying to concoct a
oncentration; if I am focused
or me to focus on my guests.
se perfect hostesses (every-
tance, who effortlessly throw
essing all around them with
se of humor, and generally
n't seem to struggle in the
ter, then, gives a few ideas
asy to prepare, but which are
c, making you look super-
aving you to enjoy the party.

BACON AND CHIVE MINI-RÖSTIS

———

(makes approximately 24 röstis) *2 lbs potatoes ~ 3 tbsp olive oil ~ ½ lb smoked lardons in tiny dice ~ 2 onions, grated ~ 1 tsp salt ~ 1 tsp pepper ~ 2 large handfuls of chives, finely chopped ~ butter, for greasing* **TO SERVE:** *sour cream*

These are perfect little snacks to serve up at a party. You will ideally need a couple of mini-tart trays (each for a dozen tarts) to cook your röstis in, though otherwise, you can shape them and cook them on a baking sheet instead.

Milton's Method ☞ Parboil the potatoes whole in a large saucepan of water for 10–12 minutes until they are slightly cooked but still firm. Put them in the fridge to cool.

Add a little olive oil to a frying pan and cook the diced lardons until just starting to golden. Drain and set aside on paper towels. Preheat your oven to 450°F.

Once the potatoes have cooled, peel them and grate them into a large bowl. Add the cooked lardons, grated onion, the remaining olive oil, the salt, pepper, and all but a tablespoon or so of the chives, which you should reserve for the garnish.

Mix all the ingredients thoroughly.

Grease the tart trays, if you are using, or your baking sheet, and place the potato mixture in each section, pressing firmly down so that each rösti is well compacted. If using a baking sheet, place a small handful of the potato mixture between the palms of your hands and press together until it is well compacted. Place on the baking sheet and bake for about 30 minutes or until golden brown.

Serve garnished with a dollop of sour cream, chives, and some freshly ground black pepper on top.

BAKED CAMEMBERT

WITH ROSEMARY, THYME, AND SOLDIERS

A whole 8.8-oz circular Camembert in a wooden box ~ 6–8 small sprigs of rosemary ~ large pinch of fresh thyme ~ pepper ~ 1 ciabatta loaf, sliced into chunky strips about 4 x 1-inch each ~ 2 tbsp olive oil ~ handful of chopped fresh chives **TO SERVE:** *apple slices ~ grapes ~ onion chutney*

A warm, rich, meltingly soft Camembert has the kind of oozy consistency that is best eaten with crunchy sticks of bread baked with olive oil—a grown-up version of sticking soldiers in your boiled egg. The herbs give the dish a wonderful aroma. If your bread is stale, so much the better.

Cooking doesn't get any simpler than this.

Milton's Method ☞ Preheat the oven to 350°F. Remove any plastic packaging from the Camembert, line the wooden box with a little parchment paper, and put the cheese back in.

Score several slits across the top of the cheese with a sharp knife and poke in the rosemary sprigs. Sprinkle the thyme and a couple of grinds of black pepper over the top. Place on a baking sheet.

Prepare the bread by brushing each "soldier" all over with olive oil and placing on a baking sheet. Bake the cheese and the bread in the oven for 15–20 minutes, or until the center of the cheese has melted and the bread is crisp and golden.

Sprinkle the chives over the cheese and serve immediately with thin wedges of tart eating apples, grapes, and onion chutney.

BRUSCHETTA

WITH OLIVES
AND ANCHOVIES

—

(makes approximately 25 bruschette) *1 French baguette, cut into ¼-inch-thick slices ~ 4 tbsp good-quality olive oil ~ 3 cloves garlic, finely chopped ~ 1 14.5-oz can diced tomatoes ~ approx. 35 green olives, thinly sliced ~ approx. 25 white anchovy fillets ~ salt and pepper*

All the best accompaniments to drinking are salty, and this is no exception—crispy, baked baguettes topped with a garlicky tomato sauce, anchovies, and olives. Super simple and super tasty.

Milton's Method ☞ Preheat the oven to 325°F. Brush the slices of bread with olive oil and place on a baking sheet. Bake for about 10 minutes, until lightly toasted. Be careful not to overcook.

Place a frying pan on medium heat and pour in the rest of the olive oil. Add the garlic and cook for a minute or so, stirring, until it is just beginning to change color. Add the tomatoes and stir well. Season to taste. Turn the heat down and simmer for 20 minutes, stirring occasionally. The liquid will reduce and the tomatoes will become a thick paste.

Spread the paste on the bruschetta and top with the sliced olives and a single piece of anchovy per slice.

CROSTINI

WITH TUNA AND
CAPER BERRIES

———

(makes approximately 24 crostini) *1 baguette, sliced into ¼-inch pieces ~ 2 tbsp olive oil ~ 1½ 5-oz cans pole-caught tuna in olive oil ~ 6 canned anchovy fillets ~ 2 tbsp capers ~ 1 tbsp grated lemon zest ~ 1 clove garlic ~ ⅓ cup mascarpone cheese ~ handful of kalamata olives, pitted and halved ~ handful of parsley, roughly chopped ~ 24 caper berries*

Yes, caper berries are those things that you only ever normally see at drinks receptions and parties when a real person isn't picking up the tab. And these are the kind of smart canapé (if slightly on the larger side) that you might see at such a do. I'm not entirely sure if there is a difference between crostini and bruschetta, but this one is crostini. Definitely. At least, I definitely think so.

Milton's Method ☞ Preheat the oven to 325°F. Brush the slices of bread on both sides with olive oil and place on a baking sheet. Bake for about 10 minutes, but be careful not to overcook them.

Combine all the other ingredients except for the caper berries in a blender, including the oil from the tuna. Blitz into a smooth paste.

When you're almost ready to serve the crostini (do it too early and they'll lose their crispness), spread the mixture on the bread and top each slice with a caper berry.

"One should always
be drunk. That's
all that matters . . .
But with what? With
wine, with poetry,
or with virtue, as you
choose. But get drunk."

Charles Baudelaire

ENGLISH CHEESE FONDUE

WITH PERRY

—

1 lb of a mixture of coarsely grated cheese such as aged cheddar, Cheshire, Red Leicester, and Double Gloucester ~ ½ tsp Colman's mustard powder ~ ¾ cup medium dry perry (e.g., Hogan's Vintage Perry) ~ 2 tsp cornstarch ~ 2 tbsp light cream ~ 1 tbsp cider brandy or pear brandy (or French brandy if you have neither of these) ~ pepper **TO SERVE:** *ingredients for dipping e.g. whole wheat toast, gherkins, pickled cauliflower, apple slices, and celery stalks*

After a hard day of work (or play), a fondue is a great thing to share with friends. Hell, let's get cheesy as anything and call it a "fun-do," because you can't help but have a cartoon grin on your face when you're eating it. It is possible to make a great fondue using English, rather than French or Swiss, cheeses and English perry (a hard cider made with pears), rather than white wine, which is what I have done here.

This is best if you have an alcohol burner that you can place on a table with a fondue pot or saucepan on top as you need to keep the fondue warm to prevent it from solidifying.

Milton's Method ☞ Toss the cheese with the mustard powder and set aside to reach room temperature.

Pour the perry into a saucepan and heat to just before boiling point. Remove from the heat and tip in half of the cheese. Stir the cheese into the perry with a wooden spoon, using a backward and forward motion rather than a circular one to avoid splitting the mixture.

Return the saucepan to low heat, stirring all the time. Add the remaining cheese gradually until it is all melted. Mix the cornstarch with the cream and add it to the mixture, then stir to thicken. Add the brandy and season with pepper. Transfer the saucepan to the burner or pour the mixture into the fondue pot.

Serve with bite-size chunks of whole wheat toast or bread rolls, gherkins, pickled cauliflower, segments of apple, sticks of celery, and anything else you fancy, using fondue forks if you have them, or skewers if you don't.

STEAK HACHÉ SLIDERS

ON TOASTED BRIOCHE

(makes 12 sliders) *1⅓ lbs ground sirloin with good fat content (not too lean) ~ salt and pepper ~ olive oil, for brushing ~ 1-lb loaf sliced brioche ~ red onion chutney* **TO SERVE:** *12 small slices bleu d'Auvergne* **YOU WILL NEED:** *circular pastry cutter, approx. 2½ inches in diameter ~ cocktail sticks*

The quality of the end product here depends entirely on the quality of the meat. There are no tricks or gimmicks with steak haché—unlike a burger, it is just pure beef.

A slider is a small burger, much loved of restaurants with high margins. The advantage when making sliders yourself is that they make ideal party food, rather than a meal in itself. Here, the quantities are for a dozen sliders: two dozen morsels of sweet brioche, sandwiched together with savory meat, sharp blue cheese, and slightly acidic chutney.

Milton's Method ☞ In a large bowl, season the meat well with salt and pepper and mix in with your hands. Using a circular pastry cutter placed on a plate, press the meat down inside it to a depth of ¾–1 inch. Make 12 patties this way.

Place some oil in a small bowl and brush each steak patty with oil on the upper side. Heat a cast-iron skillet and, when it's very hot, add your sliders, oiled side down, pressing down a little with the back of a metal slice. While they're cooking, brush the other side with oil.

Brush the brioche with olive oil and toast under a broiler until golden then, using the pastry cutter, cut the brioche to the same size as the burgers. Spread onion chutney on one side of 12 toasted brioche slices.

For rare, cook your patties for 2–3 minutes on each side so that they're just seared on the outside. A medium burger will be about 5 minutes per side.

Place the burgers on top of the chutney side of the brioche, add a slice of bleu d'Auvergne to each, put the hat of the slider on top, and skewer with a cocktail stick to keep in place.

BOOZY
DESSERTS

—

Alcohol and desse
marriage. Desserts
and what could be
pouring a few units
already fantastica
course? Even if you
your actual dessert
the option of havin
range of drinks with i
the appearance of
digestifs is the sign o
well and is ending o

s make a perfect
offer us indulgence,
more indulgent than
of alcohol over your
unhealthy final
on't add alcohol to
then there is always
one of an enormous
or after it, or both:
dessert wines and
a meal that has gone
he best possible note.

CRÊPES
TOM FOSTER

—

FOR THE CRÊPES: *¼ cup flour ~ pinch of salt ~ 1 egg ~ ½ cup milk ~ 2½ tbsp water ~ 2 tbsp butter* **FOR THE BANANAS:** *3½ tbsp butter ~ ½ cup soft brown sugar ~ ½ tsp ground cinnamon ~ 4 tbsp banana liqueur (Bols or De Kuyper) ~ 4 bananas, peeled, topped, and tailed, and cut lengthwise into 4 segments ~ 4 tbsp dark rum* **TO SERVE:** *vanilla ice cream*

Bananas, at least to my mind, need a bit of booze and sugar and spice to make them nice. Bananas Foster, named after a member of the New Orleans crime commission from the 1950s, Richard Foster, is a great staple recipe from the New Orleans Brennan's Restaurant. The French culture that left so great a mark on New Orleans suggested another possible variation on this dessert to me—turning the bananas into a filling for crêpes that I've decided to name after my great friend—and Francophile—Tom Foster.

Milton's Method ☞ Make the batter for the crêpes by sifting the flour and salt into a large bowl and making a well in the center. Break the egg into the well and whisk it with a fork, gradually incorporating the flour. Mix the milk and the water together and add them to the flour gradually, incorporating all the flour and whisking with the fork until the batter is smooth. Rest the batter in the fridge for about 15 minutes.

For the banana mixture, heat a frying pan over medium heat, add the butter, sugar, and cinnamon and cook until the sugar has dissolved and the sauce is a deep caramel color. Add the banana liqueur and the banana pieces. Move the banana pieces around the pan until they start to color. Add the rum and, carefully, tilt the pan to flambé (flame) the liqueur. Mind your eyebrows! Take the pan off the heat and set it aside.

In a separate frying pan, melt some butter over medium-high heat. Pour a ladleful of batter into it, quickly swirling the pan so it spreads as thinly as possible across the bottom of the pan.

Cook the crêpe for 45 seconds to 1 minute before flipping to cook the other side. Don't bother turning it with a spatula. Flip it. It's worth taking a risk or two in life. Cook for another 30–45 seconds until golden and remove from the pan to a warmed plate. Add some more butter and repeat.

When the crêpes are ready, fill with the banana mixture and serve with ice cream.

CARAMELIZED RUM MANGO

WITH VODKA LIME JELL-O AND GINGERSNAP CRUMBLE

—

1 package lime Jell-O ~ vodka, to taste ~ 4 tbsp sugar ~ 1 tbsp dark rum ~ 1 tbsp water ~ 1 vanilla pod, halved and seeds scraped out ~ 1 mango, peeled, cored, and sliced ~ 2 tsp lime juice ~ 4 gingersnap cookies, lightly crushed

Tropical fruits have always been one of my favorite things about visiting warmer climes, and this boozy tropical fruit treat couldn't be simpler to make. Remember that the Jell-O needs to be made in advance to have time to set. And, remember too, that vodka Jell-O can get you extremely drunk, so use with caution!

Milton's Method ☞ Follow the package instructions to make the lime Jell-O, but only use two-thirds the recommended amount of boiling water, then, once the Jell-O has dissolved, top up with the vodka. Depending on the strength you want, you can change the ratio of vodka to water. Pour the liquid Jell-O into ice cube molds and place in the fridge to set.

Once the Jell-O has set, prepare the mango by heating the sugar, rum, water, and vanilla seeds in a nonstick saucepan over medium heat. It should come to a boil within a couple of minutes and begin to reduce and get sticky. Add the mango and make sure that all of it is coated in the caramel mixture as it continues to reduce. Take care not to burn the caramel. Once the mango is heated through and well coated with the mixture, remove the saucepan from the heat.

Place the mango on a plate, spooning any additional caramel over it. Squeeze a little lime juice over the top to freshen it up. Place a couple of cubes of lime Jell-O on the plate and sprinkle the gingersnap crumble on the mango.

Eat while the mango is still warm.

MILTON'S
TIPSY TRIFLE

 (cinch)

1 package raspberry Jell-O ~ 1¾ cups frozen summer fruits ~ 1 piece star anise ~ 3 tbsp sugar ~ 16–20 lady's fingers ~ 4 tbsp blackcurrant jam ~ ½ cup sweet sherry ~ 1⅓ cups thick ready-made custard ~ 1 cup heavy cream ~ toasted sliced almonds

There are few things more British than a trifle soaked in sherry with thick custard and cream and summer fruits (even though this recipe is made with French lady's fingers). I've used thick, ready-made fresh custard in the recipe as the tedium of making it myself was too much to bear. If you are less lazy than I, then by all means start cracking those eggs. This trifle should be served in a glass dish so that you can see the layers.

Milton's Method ☞ Make the Jell-O according to the package instructions. Place in the freezer to set. Thaw the summer fruits in a small saucepan over low heat with the star anise and the sugar. Stir a couple of times. When thawed, after 5 minutes, remove the star anise and allow the fruits to cool.

Layer half the lady's fingers on the bottom of a small glass serving dish so that the surface is covered, then spread the jam over the top. Add another layer of lady's fingers then pour the sherry over the top. Add the summer fruits mix, then a layer of custard. Break up the Jell-O and spread it on top of the custard then layer more custard on top. Whip the cream until thick then layer it over the custard and garnish with the sliced almonds.

Leave in the fridge to set for 1–2 hours before serving.

PANETTONE

WITH PEDRO XIMÉNEZ, RAISINS,
ALMONDS, AND ICE CREAM

(cinch)

*2 large slices of panettone ~ ½ cup Pedro Ximénez
~ 1 tbsp soft brown sugar ~ squeeze of lemon juice
~ 2 large scoops of good-quality vanilla ice cream ~
1 tbsp golden raisins ~ handful of blanched, peeled
almonds*

I admit to not being an expert in panettone, so it may be that the varieties I've been given as gifts have not been the best, but I've often found them to be overly dry and airy. My handy solution to this problem—as is often the case in a crisis—has been to soak the thing in booze. I'm not too fussy about this and generally have used whatever I've got lying around at the time. This has included marsala, dark rum, brandy, and, memorably, sloe gin, but the best booze to use to make a great dessert out of panettone, without a doubt, is Pedro Ximénez, or "PX"—sweet, dark, raisin-y sherry.

Milton's Method ☞ Place the slices
of panettone in 2 serving bowls
and pour the Pedro Ximénez over
them. Leave to soak. Combine
the brown sugar and the lemon
juice in a separate bowl. Mix well.

Spoon the ice cream on top of the
panettone, then dribble the lemon
juice and sugar mixture on top of
the ice cream. Sprinkle the raisins
and the almonds over the top and
serve immediately.

SHERRY AND GINGER LOG

WITH PISTACHIO AND CHOCOLATE

———

1⅓ cups heavy cream ~ ½ cup medium dry sherry ~ 30 gingersnap cookies ~ 2 tbsp pistachio nuts, shelled and roughly chopped ~ 1 tbsp crystallized stem ginger, roughly chopped ~ 3 oz good-quality dark chocolate, shaved

This is a retro treat that my dear mother used to cook, back in the days when people still believed that heavy cream was a healthy snack. I actually do think that heavy cream is healthy so long as it's eaten in the right proportion with everything else. One of my mottos is to never, ever, choose low-fat varieties of anything when a full-fat one is available: the full-fat one is always much tastier.

This dessert should be prepared in advance and chilled in the fridge for a few hours to set.

Milton's Method ☞ In a large mixing bowl, whisk the cream until thickened and stiff. Fold 2 tablespoons of the sherry into the cream. Smear a line of cream down the center of a serving plate. This will hold your confection in place.

Pour the remaining sherry into a small bowl. Dunk the cookies into the sherry one by one. This has to be judged carefully—dip too briefly and your cookie will not soak up enough sherry. Dip for too long and your cookie will disintegrate. I recommend something along the lines of: dip—one-elephant, two-elephant—and remove. After you have dunked one cookie, spread some of the cream on one side with an offset spatula. Repeat this process, sticking the cookies together with the cream and placing them on the plate until you have a "log" shape.

Spread the remaining cream carefully and evenly over the entire log. Place in the fridge for 2–3 hours to set. Remove from the fridge and garnish with the pistachios, stem ginger, and chocolate shavings.

Et voilà! Serve.

THE BIG
LEBOWSKI
SUNDAE

—

4 ice cubes ~ 4 tbsp Kahlúa ~ 4 tbsp chilled vodka ~ 4 scoops vanilla ice cream ~ 1 14-oz can condensed milk ~ 1 tbsp toasted crushed hazelnuts ~ 2 maraschino cherries

Based on a classic white Russian cocktail, this is the kind of alcoholic ice-cream sundae that The Dude might approve of. It should have a strikingly layered effect with the coffee-colored Kahlúa at the bottom and the condensed milk and ice cream at the top. If you muddle the ingredients together it becomes something else entirely (a "dirty bird"), which may or may not suit you, depending on your proclivities and your mood.

Milton's Method ☞ Take 2 chilled sundae glasses, or any other type of tall, slender glass that you might have at hand, and put the ice cubes, Kahlúa, and vodka in them. Carefully place a scoop of ice cream in each so that it doesn't fall into the bottom of the glass but rests on top of the ice cubes, distinct from the dark Kahlúa layer beneath.

Pour in condensed milk almost to the top of each glass. Add another scoop of ice cream, sprinkle with the toasted, crushed hazelnuts, add a teaspoon of Kahlúa for color, and top with a maraschino cherry to garnish.

VITTLES
AND VINE

—

Matching food and drink
each and is all the rage th
but also beer, cider, anc
marketeers look for eve
per-suade us to part with
number of these matching e
industry manufacturers an
this book, dear reader. The
Indian food" and "wh
late." And, however cyn
their motives, and howe
to the most egregious forn
occasionally revelatory: e
a few pairings that I hope
you to experiment witl

n add a new dimension to
e days, not just with wine
ven whisky, as the booze
more inventive ways to
ur cash. I have been to a
nts orchestrated by drinks
retailers as research for
ncluded "beer pairings with
ky pairings with choco-
l I may have been about
r tired I got of listening
of bullshit, the results were
hanies of taste. Here are
l inspire you and encourage
your own combinations.

A SIMPLIFIED ARNOLD BENNETT OMELETTE

WITH WHITE BURGUNDY

—

 (toil)

½ lb smoked haddock, skin on ~ 1 cup milk ~ 1 bay leaf ~ 12 peppercorns ~ 5 eggs ~ ½ cup crème fraîche ~ small handful of tarragon, finely chopped ~ small handful of chives, finely chopped ~ knob of butter ~ 3 oz grated Parmesan ~ salt and pepper **TO SERVE:** *2 handfuls of watercress*

The Food

This has a reputation of a rather difficult dish for the average domestic cook, but when stripped back to its basics—a creamy, cheesy, smoked-fish omelette—it certainly doesn't have to be, and I have simplified my version of it as much as possible by eliminating the complex sauces. While something may be lost in doing this, remember: this dish was developed by chefs at London's Savoy hotel. And let's face it, not all of us want to faff around pretending to be on *MasterChef* when there's fun to be had outside the kitchen. I have also added tarragon to give it a more distinctively French flavor that seems doubly appropriate when matched with white Burgundy.

Milton's Method ☞ Poach the haddock by simmering it in the milk in a saucepan with the bay leaf and the peppercorns for 8–10 minutes. Remove from the pan, drain well, and flake the fish from the skin onto a plate, checking for bones, and set aside.

Separate one of your eggs, reserving the yolk for the omelette, and whisk the egg white in a bowl until you have soft peaks, then gradually fold in the crème fraîche and the tarragon. Set aside while you make the omelette. Whisk the remaining eggs in a bowl and season with salt, pepper, and chives. Add the knob of butter to a heavy frying pan over medium-high heat and, when melted and beginning to bubble, add the eggs to the pan. Use a spatula to stop the omelette from sticking to the sides and cook until there is just a little residual runniness on the top.

Scatter the flaked haddock on top and pour the whisked egg white and crème fraîche mixture over the fish so it covers the entire omelette. Cover with the Parmesan and place under a hot broiler until golden brown. Serve with watercress and a glass of Burgundy.

The Drink
Many of the most famous names of French wine, including Mersault and Puligny-Montrachet, can be found in the Burgundy region between Dijon and Lyon. The white wines here are made from the chardonnay grape and go extremely well with creamy fish dishes. The only thing you'll have to watch is your wallet—Burgundy is a notoriously expensive wine.

CURRIED MONKFISH AND MUSSELS

WITH GEWÜRZTRAMINER

---

2 pieces of monkfish tail, each about 6 oz, skinned and boned ~ 3 tsp curry powder ~ salt ~ 2 leeks, washed, halved lengthwise, and chopped into semicircular pieces ~ 2 tbsp olive oil ~ pinch of saffron ~ 1 lb mussels, cleaned and with beards removed ~ ½ cup dry white wine ~ 1 bay leaf ~ 2 sprigs of thyme ~ ½ cup heavy cream ~ pepper **TO SERVE:** *French bread or mashed potatoes ~ wilted spinach*

The Food

A simple, elegant dish curried in the French style—i.e., with the simple addition of curry powder, saffron, and cream, rather than with a whole combination of deep flavors and spices. Monkfish is expensive but delicious, with a uniquely firm texture.

Milton's Method ☞ Heat the oven to 350°F. Remove the thin gray membrane from the monkfish. Dust the fillets with 2 teaspoons of the curry powder and a good pinch of salt (about ½ teaspoon). Set aside.

Sautée the leeks very gently in a little olive oil with the remaining curry powder and a pinch of saffron. Meanwhile, heat an ovenproof frying pan over medium-high heat and add a tablespoon of olive oil then the monkfish fillets. Cook for about 3 minutes, or until they have colored all over, then pop the pan into the oven for 5 minutes.

While the monkfish is in the oven, cook the mussels. Heat a deep saucepan over medium heat and add the mussels, wine, bay leaf, and thyme. Cover and shake. The mussels should take about 4 minutes to cook.

Remove the mussels from the heat (discarding any that haven't opened) and add the cooking liquor from the mussels to the pan with the leeks in it. Let the sauce reduce a little then add the cream and season with salt and pepper. Stir thoroughly and simmer on low heat for a couple of minutes while you assemble the other ingredients. Remove the bay leaf.

The fish is ready when it's firm to the touch. Remove it from the oven and set aside. If you have time, and you want your plate to look smart, remove the mussels from their shells. Pour the creamy leek sauce into shallow bowls, add the fish, and scatter the mussels around it. Serve either with some warm French bread to mop up the sauce or creamy mashed potatoes and wilted spinach.

The Drink
Gewürztraminer is a wonderfully fruity and aromatic white wine that is most popularly associated with the Alsace region of France, though good examples can also be found from Chile, New Zealand, and North America. It is commonly paired with spicy dishes and works especially well with the cream, saffron, and the curry powder in this recipe.

SALT COD CROQUETTES

WITH MANZANILLA

———

¾ lb salt cod fillet ~ 2 cups milk ~ ½ onion, sliced ~ a few peppercorns ~ 1 bay leaf ~ ⅔ cup mashed potatoes ~ handful of parsley, finely chopped ~ 2 tsp lemon juice ~ ½ cup all-purpose flour ~ 2 eggs, beaten ~ 1 cup fine white bread crumbs ~ vegetable oil, for frying ~ salt and pepper **TO SERVE:** *garlic mayonnaise ~ arugula*

The Food
Salt cod is dry and needs to be rehydrated and desalted. Soak it for 24 hours before use, in several changes of water. The croquettes are a common tapas dish in Spain and make great drinking food: crispy on the outside, moist and salty within.

Milton's Method ☞ Poach the cod in the milk (see page 131) with the sliced onion, peppercorns, and bay leaf for 15 minutes, then gently flake the fish into a bowl, removing any bones.

Combine the mashed potatoes, cod, parsley, and lemon juice in a large bowl and season generously to taste. Break the mixture into several small balls—you should get 8–10. Then elongate slightly so you have something like small, rounded cylinders. Roll in the flour, then in the beaten egg, and finally in the bread crumbs. Heat ¾ inch of vegetable oil in a frying pan over medium-high heat, and when hot, add the croquettes and fry until golden and crisp. Serve with garlic mayonnaise and arugula.

The Drink
Manzanilla is a type of dry fino sherry that's perfect with fish. It is produced near the sea and there is an element of saltiness to it (it is often described as "briny") that especially lends itself to drinking with seafood.

"I cook with
wine, sometimes
I even add
it to the food."

W.C. Fields

SEARED SCALLOPS, SMOKED LARDONS, AND BLOOD SAUSAGE

WITH PORTER

---

8 scallops (4 per person), including "coral" ~ salt and pepper ~ knob of butter ~ 8 rounds of blood sausage, about ½ inch thick ~ 4 oz smoked lardons ~ large handful of arugula ~ juice of 1 lemon ~ drizzle of extra virgin olive oil

The Food

Scallops have become one of the most essential of all ingredients in fashionable modern gastronomy. There is good reason for it—at their best they're sweet, juicy, and delicious. Smoked lardons, blood sausage, and a few arugula leaves here provide the perfect foil.

Milton's Method ☞ Pat the scallops dry with some paper towels and season well with salt and pepper. Melt a generous knob of butter in a heavy frying pan on high heat and sear the blood sausage on both sides. Put on a warm plate and set aside.

Cook the lardons in the same pan until crisp and golden. Drain on paper towels. Now sear the scallops—about 90 seconds on one side, 30 seconds on the other. They should be golden on the surface. The coral should be opaque and firm to the touch.

Arrange the scallops on a plate with the blood sausage. Sprinkle the lardons and the arugula over them. Deglaze the pan with the lemon juice, add a little olive oil, and drizzle the pan juices over the top of the scallops. Serve straightaway.

The Drink

Porter is a dark, rich, complex beer that's usually fairly strong—between 5 and 6.5%. It is an excellent match for scallops and oysters. Two good examples are Fuller's London Porter and Meantime London Porter.

STUFFED GRILLED MUSSELS

WITH INNIS AND
GUNN BLONDE

---

24 mussels, cleaned and debearded ~ ¼ cup dry sherry ~ ¼ cup butter ~
1 shallot, finely diced ~ ½ cup all-purpose flour ~ 1 cup milk ~ ½ cup white
wine ~ handful of parsley, finely chopped ~ ¼ cup fresh bread crumbs ~ 2 oz
finely grated Parmesan ~ salt and pepper

The Food
Buy the biggest mussels you can find for this recipe—succulent
mussels in their shell with a creamy sauce and a crisp Parmesan
crust on top.

Milton's Method ☞ Cook the mussels in a saucepan with the sherry
and the lid on. This takes just 3 minutes. Remove the pan from the
heat and discard any mussels that haven't opened.

In another pan melt the butter and cook the shallot over medium
heat. When the shallot has softened, add the flour and stir in. Cook
for a minute then add the milk gradually, stirring constantly to remove
any lumps. When all the milk is incorporated, and the sauce has
thickened a little, add the wine. Cook for another 5–7 minutes,
until the alcohol has evaporated and the sauce is thickened and almost
gooey. Season to taste. Add the parsley.

Remove and discard the upper shell of each mussel. Place the
mussels on a baking sheet and spoon a little sauce onto each.

Combine the bread crumbs and the Parmesan and sprinkle over
the mussels. Place under a hot broiler until the bread crumbs have
turned crisp and golden.

The Drink

Innis and Gunn Blonde is a pale, golden beer that is aged in oak barrels. The flavor is quite unlike that of any other beer that I have tasted. The first time I tried it was with oysters and it was a perfect fit. Toffee and vanilla are underscored by malt, oak, and citrus, which together provide a perfect match for shellfish.

VENISON SAUSAGES

WITH CIDER SAUCE
AND SCRUMPY

___

2 tbsp olive oil ~ 2 onions, roughly chopped ~ 2 large eating apples, peeled and roughly chopped ~ ½ butternut squash, peeled and roughly chopped ~ 6 good-quality venison sausages ~ 1 tbsp thyme, roughly chopped ~ 2 sprigs of rosemary ~ salt and pepper ~ 1 tbsp all-purpose flour ~ ¾ cup hard cider ~ ½ cup chicken stock **TO SERVE:** *mashed potatoes ~ kale, spinach, or sprouts*

The Food

I've spent a fair bit of time living in the New Forest in southern England and this simple recipe represents some of the flavors from the area that mean the most to me, mainly venison, hard cider, and apples.

Milton's Method ☞ Heat your oven to 425°F. Warm some olive oil in a roasting pan and keep the pan over medium heat as you add the onions, apple, squash, sausages, thyme, and rosemary. Season generously with salt and pepper. Shake everything about reasonably vigorously. When everything is well coated with oil and seasoning, place the roasting pan in the mid/upper part of the oven and cook for 30–40 minutes, turning the sausages once or twice.

When everything is cooked, the squash and onions should just be beginning to caramelize and the sausages should be well browned. Set the sausages aside in a warm place and put three quarters of the vegetables in a warm serving dish. Remove the sprigs of rosemary.

To make a gravy, place the roasting pan on the stove over low heat, add the flour to the fat at the bottom of the pan and stir it in until it is well blended in and you have a pale-looking paste. Mash some of the squash and apple into the mix as you go. Add a little of the cider and stir vigorously into the paste, until it thickens. Keep adding

cider, making sure that the cider is well
absorbed and the liquid thickens. Once all the
cider has been added, bring quickly to a boil and simmer
for a minute or two, stirring all the while, before adding the stock.
Bring back up to a boil again and let it simmer for 10 minutes,
stirring occasionally, reducing and thickening. If the gravy gets too
thick, add a little water. Strain through a colander, mashing the
vegetables through. Serve the sausages with the vegetables, gravy,
mashed potatoes, and greens like kale, spinach, or sprouts.

The Drink

Proper scrumpy always has a homemade feel to it. You should almost
be able to taste the hay in the barn in which it was made. Unlike
many mass-market commercial ciders, it should taste of apples. It
might be cloudy and vary in hue from pale yellow to bright orange.
It should be strong—at least 6% ABV. My favorite color of scrumpy is
the kind of gold that the trees sometimes turn in autumn—a deep,
rich color that's somewhere between a setting sun and sunlight
through a brackish stream. I have made my own scrumpy very
successfully, and if you have a ready supply of apples I suggest you try
it too (please refer to disclaimers at various points in this book).

I have drunk plenty of a New Forest cider referred to as "Tight Hat
Cider" by the maker's son. He says: "After a couple of pints of it,
I feel like I'm wearing a very tight hat." This is proper scrumpy: stuff
that has strange, unquantifiable properties and that may make you
do unexpected things. Like the wobbly-leg cider I had in Wiltshire.
Or that stuff in Sussex I tried where I got naked and found myself
hiding . . . Oh, but wait, that's another story. For another time.

Acknowledgments

Thanks to all my drinking companions, past and present, who have helped, however unwittingly, in the creation of this book. It is a long list so I shan't mention all of them. They know who they are.

Particular thanks to my agent, Andrew Gordon, and his assistant, Marigold Atkey, at David Higham Associates, and to Rosemary Davidson and Simon Rhodes at Random House, for all their hard work in helping this book to publication.

Thanks also to all those who tried, tested, and suggested recipes, including Simon and Rosalind Gould, Henry Riley and Lisa Brackenridge, Anna and Tommy Macken, Jimmy and Tomo Robertson, Helen and Chris Davis and Sue and Steve Telfer, Michael and Billi Ksela, and Wolfgang Ritter.

It has been a pleasure working with the very talented illustrators and designers Katie Morgan, Matt Baxter, and Graeme Rodrigo, who have made this book as beautiful as it is.

Last, but quite the opposite from the least, thanks to Bridget and Gilbert for all their love and support.

Final Disclaimer

Please get drunk responsibly. And know your limits. Especially in the kitchen.

We (the author and publisher) will not accept any responsibility for your drunken condition or your experimentation in the kitchen (based on the contents of this book or otherwise), nor for any implications for your health arising thereof.

The author has thoroughly researched all the recipes in this book and, to the best of his knowledge, believes the ingredients, quantities, and methods to be entirely correct. He will not accept responsibility for any attempts at his recipes that fail.

We wish you the best of luck. You may well need it.

All about Milton

Milton Crawford made a name for himself with *The Hungover Cookbook* (2010), which brought him global notoriety, and soon after (in 2011) he was named the Bombardier Beer Writer of the Year. His passion for alcohol is matched by his love of food, travel, pubs, and the outdoors. He finds that a strict regimen of exercise helps him to drink and eat greater amounts, recover faster, and come back for more sooner; this regime was, at least in part, inspired by the 2012 London Olympics. Thanks, Sebastian.

He believes, along with Baudelaire, that intoxication is an essential precondition of creative life. Alcohol is not entirely necessary for this, but for those lacking in imagination and means, it is the most readily available vehicle.

Milton divides his time between London, the New Forest, Austria, and India, hoping that if he is able to spread himself thinly enough across enough of the planet, he will merge into some higher form of consciousness. This has not happened yet.

Milton stopped tweeting @miltoncrawford (as he tweeted using the same hand as he was using to hold his glass, and it all got too much) but may start again at some point in the future.